lonely planet

POCKET
MUNICH

Marc Di Duca

Contents

Top: Oktoberfest (p134)
Bottom: The Altstadt (p35)

Plan Your Trip   4

The Journey Begins Here 4
Our Picks 6
Perfect Days 18
Get Prepared 22
When To Go 24
Getting There 26
Getting Around 27
A Few Surprises 30

POCKET **MUNICH**

Explore Munich   33

Altstadt & the Residenz 35
Maxvorstadt 61
Schwabing & the
Englischer Garten 81
Haidhausen, Lehel & Au 101
Nymphenburg, BMW
& Olympiapark 115

Munich Toolkit   141

Family Travel 142
Accommodation 143
Food, Drink & Nightlife 144
LGBTIQ+ Travellers 146
Health & Safe Travel 147
Responsible Travel 148
Accessible Travel 150
Nuts & Bolts 151
Language 152
Index 154

★ Top Experiences

Munich Residenz 38
Marienplatz 42
Asamkirche 44
Frauenkirche 46
Hofbräuhaus 47
Kunstareal 64
NS Dokuzentrum 70
Englischer Garten 84
Ludwig-Maximilians-
Universität 88
Bayerisches
Nationalmuseum 89
Deutsches Museum 104
Museum Villa Stuck 106
Sudetendeutsches Museum ... 107
Olympiapark 118
The BMW Experience 123
Schloss Nymphenburg 127
Oktoberfest 134

Worth a Trip

KZ-Gedenkstätte Dachau 78
Schleissheim Palaces 96
Schloss Neuschwanstein 98
Lake Starnberg 138

PLAN YOUR TRIP

The Journey Begins Here

World-class art and thigh-slapping tradition, bamboozling technology and Europe's finest beer, head-turning architecture and high-octane affluence – Munich certainly keeps its central European promises, all infused with Bavarian *Gemütlichkeit,* that untranslatable feeling of cosiness and wellbeing. One of Europe's most eclectic destinations, there's truly something for everyone in Germany's secret capital.

Marc Di Duca
@marcdiduca
Marc has been a travel guide author for the past two decades, penning almost 200 guides to places as diverse as Brazil and Siberia for Lonely Planet and most other major travel publishers. He currently lives with his family on the Czech-Bavarian border.

The Altstadt (p35)
MP_FOTO/SHUTTERSTOCK

PLAN YOUR TRIP

THE BEST
Beer Garden Experiences

A night in a fairy-lit beer garden in the company of one of Munich's big six breweries and some belly-filling food is a quintessential Munich experience. Here we list the best.

Join a small army of drinkers at the **Hirschgarten** near Schloss Nymphenburg, the world's largest beer garden. (p133)

Raise a toast to the **Chinesischer Turm** (pictured above right), Munich's most enjoyable beer garden gathered around a Chinese tower folly. (p85)

Head south to Au and the **Paulaner am Nockherberg**, with its modern styling and great food. (p113)

Go for something slightly different at the **Biergarten Muffatwerk**, where health-conscious food but the same plentiful beer are served. (p113)

Take one of the 5000 seats at the **Augustiner Keller**, a firm favourite with fans of Augustiner lager. (p77)

Imbibe as you watch the kids play at **Hirschau** in the north of the Englischer Garten. (p95)

Right: Food options at Hirshau (p95)

FROM LEFT: REGULA WOLF, ARTIMENTE/SHUTTERSTOCK, DIE DESIGNERIE/JANIKA BUBELA

THE BEST

Art Experiences

It is no exaggeration to say that Munich can boast the finest art collections in central Europe and has an entire neighbourhood – the Kunstareal – dedicated to genres of all kinds.

Visit the **Alte Pinakothek**, for many the definite highlight of the Kunstareal with its austere building and vast collection of old masters. (p64)

Whirl around the **Museum Brandhorst**, Munich's showcase for 20th-century and contemporary art. (p65)

Tick off three museums in one at **Pinakothek der Moderne** (pictured above), where 20th-century cars sit alongside Picassos. (p66)

Take in a touring show at the **Haus der Kunst** (pictured above), a gallery built by Hitler which now showcases the very art the Nazis shunned. (p92)

Learn about the Blue Rider movement at the Kunstareal's **Lenbachhaus**, a historic villa and contemporary underground extension. (p68)

Right: Alte Pinakothek (p64)

FROM LEFT: © BAYERISCHE STAATSGEMÄLDESAMMLUNGEN, TOM VACK, WWW.SCHLOSSER.BAYERN.DE, MAXIMILIAN GEUTER, © BAYERISCHE STAATSGEMÄLDESAMMLUNGEN, HAYDAR KOYUPINA, WWW.SCHLOSSER.BAYERN.DE

THE BEST

Beer Hall Experiences

A night in a cosy Bavarian tavern caressing a 1L tankard of some of the world's finest lager as the crimson-faced crowds sway to the oompah band is an experience you won't want to miss.

Marvel at the mothership of beer halls, the **Hofbräuhaus** (pictured above), a traditional tavern and tourist attraction rolled into one. (p47)

Experience the *Weisswurst* breakfast in the Altstadt at the **Weisses Bräuhaus**, a tavern famous for its wheat beer. (p50)

Enjoy some tranquil drinking at **Braunauer Hof**, a virtually tourist-free spot despite a city-centre location. (p57)

Choose between a wood-panelled tavern and Munich's first-ever beer garden at the **Hofbräukeller** dominating Wiener Platz. (p113)

Take a break from the Altstadt retail frenzy at the **Augustiner Stammhaus** (pictured above), which sits amid flagship stores. (p56)

For a calmer beer hall experience try **Tegernseer Tal**, where lighter wood and a large skylight can make a bright alternative to darker taverns. (p56)

Viktualienmarkt (p53)

THE BEST

Shopping Experiences

Munich's retail offerings have depth, from vintage clothes to luxury goods, flea market finds to Christmas market baubles. It's also excellent for outdoor gear and English books.

Savour the aroma of mulled wine and gingerbread at **Christkindlmarkt** during Advent (p51).

___

Source high-quality picnic supplies or take a light lunch at the central **Viktualienmarkt**, the Altstadt's famous gourmet market. (p53)

___

Test your new kayak in the basement lake at **Globetrotter**, perhaps central Europe's best outdoor-gear shop. (p58)

Rummage through the **Flohmarkt im Olympiapark**, a large flea market in the Olympiapark car park. (p131)

___

Shop for vintage Lederhosen and Dirndl at **Holareidulijö** for that authentic Oktoberfest look. (p77)

___

Stock up on English reading material at Maxvorstadt's **Munich Readery**, one of Europe's best English-language bookstores. (p77)

THE BEST

Museum Experiences

You could spend a couple of months perusing all of Munich's museum collections – the city is said to have over 80 – with exhibitions ranging from yesteryear cars to Gothic church art.

Admire the architectural styles preferred by a long list of Wittelsbach royals at Munich's top attraction, the **Residenz**. (p38)

Factor in an entire day to do the huge **Deutsches Museum** (pictured above) justice with exhibits ranging from entire space rockets to nano particles. (p104)

Wonder at Bavaria's ability to make cars at the **BMW Museum**, where Elvis' 1950s cabriolet takes pride of place. (p124)

Lose yourself in the halls of the **Bayerisches Nationalmuseum**, an old-school museum experience. (p89)

Learn about the fate of a lost Germanic culture at the large and very well-curated **Sudetendeutsches Museum**. (p107)

Take a tour of the **Museum Villa Stuck** (pictured above), one of the finest Art Nouveau residences in Europe. (p106)

Right: Munich Residenz (p38)

FROM LEFT: DEUTSCHES MUSEUM, JANN AVERWERSER, © BAYERISCHE SCHLÖSSERVERWALTUNG, MARIA SCHERF, WWW.SCHLOESSERBAYERN.DE

THE BEST

Architecture Experiences

Architecture appreciators are sure to love what Munich serves up in brick, mortar and plaster. Neogothic, real Gothic, baroque and 21st-century – the capital of Bavaria has it all.

Be knocked sideways by the sheer amount of baroque ornamentation at the Altstadt's **Asamkirche**, Munich's most elaborate church. (p44)

Take a seat in the auditorium of the baroque **Cuvilliés-Theater** (pictured above) to admire François de Cuvilliés' ornate masterpiece. (p41)

Gaze up at the 100m-high towers of the **Frauenkirche** that dominate Munich's city-centre skyline. (p46)

Wander the limestone gravel paths of the **Königsplatz**, Ludwig I's Athens on the Isar with its many museums. (p67)

Stroll the ornate hallways, chambers and chapels of **Schloss Nymphenburg**, the royal Wittelsbach family's summer residence. (p127)

Admire the architecture of **BMW Welt** (pictured above), a dramatic structure that swirls down like a glass, steel and concrete thundercloud. (p123)

Right: Asamkirche (p44)

THE BEST
WWII Experiences

Sadly, Munich is synonymous with the rise of the Nazis and the worst excesses of Hitler's evil regime. There are several sites in and around the city that recall those dark days.

Pay your respects and learn the story of the **Dachau Concentration Camp Memorial Site** (pictured above), the first camp that set the evil standards for all future camps. (p78)

Get the lowdown on Munich's role in the rise of the Nazis at the excellent **NS Dokuzentrum** in Maxvorstadt. (p70)

Pay homage to members of the White Rose resistance movement at the **DenkStätte Weisse Rose**, in Munich's main university building. (p88)

Take a moment to remember those who died at the hands of the Nazis at the **Monument to the Victims of National Socialism** (pictured above). (p50)

Stand on the spot in front of the **Feldherrnhalle** where authorities brought an end to Hitler's Beer Hall Putsch in 1923. (p51)

FROM LEFT: RAINER VIERTLBÖCK/KZ-GEDENKSTÄTTE DACHAU, NENAD NEDOMACK/SHUTTERSTOCK

Best for Kids

Let the kiddies have free rein at the **Deutsches Museum**, a Munich attraction where you'll have to drag them out at closing time. (p104)

Bundle the little ones into the superfast lift to the top of the **Olympiaturm**, where there's a cafe, amazing views and Munich's highest geocache. (p118)

Encourage your offspring to get hands-on at the science- and biology-themed **Museum Mensch und Natur** within Schloss Nymphenburg. (p129)

Head indoors with budding marine biologists when it rains to the aquariums of **Sea Life**, one of Germany's top marine-life attractions. (p122)

Let the kids loose on the lawns and playgrounds of the **Englischer Garten**, one of Europe's largest city parks with space galore for Frisbee games and kite flying. (p84)

Best for Free

Get behind the wheel of BMW's latest hydrogenmobiles at the completely free-to-enter **BMW Welt**, Munich's top free tourist attraction. (p123)

Call in at the museum next to the now-defunct **Ost-West Friedenskirche** to learn about its creator and the romantic story behind the church. (p121)

Trek the paths and climb the hills of Munich's 1972 **Olympiapark** without parting with a single euro cent. The view from the Olympiaberg is a particularly enjoyable free attraction. (p118)

Learn about Munich's role in the rise of Hitler and the Nazis at the **NS Dokuzentrum**, a commendably free attraction. (p70)

Jog, cycle or just stroll the paths and widescreen lawns of the **Englischer Garten**, where no admission is charged to wander. (p84)

Perfect Days

Munich is as good for a day excursion as it is for a month-long stay. Here we bring you itineraries for visits of varying lengths.

Merry-go-round, Hirschau (p95)

FROM LEFT: DIE DESIGNERIE/JANIKA BUBELA, © BAYERISCHE SCHLÖSSERVERWALTUNG, RAINER HERRMANN, WWW.SCHLOSSER .BAYERN.DE, TOBIAS RANZINGER, NIKADA/GETTY IMAGES

DAY ONE

Only Have One Day?

MORNING

You can easily spend the entire morning exploring Munich's top attraction, the **Residenz** (p38; pictured above), including the **Cuvilliés-Theater** (p41).

AFTERNOON

Lunch at **Schumanns Tagesbar** (p56) then take the time to peruse the Altstadt, starting at the **Marienplatz** (p42). Climb the **St Peterskirche** (p43) tower and explore the colourful bounty at the **Viktualienmarkt** (p53).

EVENING

The perfect end to a Munich day is at a beer garden. You can gather around a Chinese pagoda folly at the **Chinesischer Turm** (p95) or watch the kids frolic in a playground at the large and leafy **Hirschau** (p95), both of which are in the **Englischer Garten** (p84).

DAY TWO

A Weekend Trip

SATURDAY
Start the weekend with a quintessentially Munich experience – the *Weisswurst* breakfast at the **Weisses Bräuhaus** (p50). Suitably fortified, head to the **Residenz** (p38) to see Munich's biggest attraction. In the afternoon head to the **BMW Welt** (p123) and the **BMW Museum** (p124) for a change of pace. End the day back at the world's most famous beer hall, the **Hofbräuhaus** (p47; pictured above).

SUNDAY
Launch your Munich Sunday with breakfast at **Cafe Luitpold** (p56) before making use of the €1 admission at various arty institutions at the **Kunstareal** (p64), perhaps interrupted by a light lunch at the cafe within the **Museum Brandhorst** (p65). In the late afternoon, head to the **Englischer Garten** (p84) to end the day with food and beer at the **Chinesischer Turm** (p95) beer garden.

DAY THREE

A Short Break

DAY ONE
The Altstadt should be your focus on day one with a tour of the **Residenz** (p38), a nose around the **Marienplatz** (p42) and lunch at the **Viktualienmarkt** (p53; pictured above) on the agenda.

DAY TWO
There's more royal grandeur to explore at **Schloss Nymphenburg** (p127), to the east of the city centre. The world's biggest beer garden, **Hirschgarten** (p133), lies nearby or head back to the city centre for dinner.

DAY THREE
Spend your third day exploring the attractions at the **Olympiapark** (p118) and the **BMW complex** (p123). If you have kids aboard, the **Deutsches Museum** (p104) will keep them occupied for hours.

If You Have More Time

With three days or more you can also explore some of the Bavarian capital's less-visited sights.

Those interested in Munich's WWII heritage can make a deep dive at the **NS Dokuzentrum** (p70) and the **Dachau concentration camp** (p78). The excellent **Sudetendeutsches Museum** (p107) also tells a fascinating story associated with WWII.

There's a lot more art than just the big galleries – one of the best must be the **Lenbachhaus** (p68).

If people watching and vintage rummaging is your thing, take half a day for the mesh of streets that is **Schwabing** (p81) and **Maxvorstadt** (p61).

With more time at the Olympiapark, track down the site of the **Ost-West Friedenskirche** (p121) and the fascinating little museum there.

Take a dip at the Art Nouveau **Müller'sches Volksbad** (p109) and in the evenings seek out less-touristy beer experiences such as the **Muffatwerk** (p113), **Park Cafe** (p76) and **Augustiner Keller** (p77) beer gardens.

NS Dokuzentrum (p70)

A City Day Trip

The classic trip from Munich is to **Schloss Neuschwanstein** (p98; pictured above), the world's most famous castle. You'll have to be up early and at the Hauptbahnhof to catch the 6.31am train to Weilheim, from where bus 931 takes you right to the foot of the castles at Hohenschwangau (a journey of 2½ hours). Having advance purchase tickets is a good idea (buy online) and you'll have plenty of time after your tour of **Neuschwanstein** and **Hohenschwangau** castles to visit the **Museum der bayerischen Könige** and grab something to eat. Trains run back to Munich from nearby Füssen which can be reached by bus or on foot (4km).

On a Rainy Day

The **Residenz** (p38) is an entirely indoor experience and can take a whole morning at least. Grab an indoor table for lunch at **Schumanns Tagesbar** (p56), which is not far away.

In the afternoon, the U-Bahn will whisk you north to the **BMW complex** (p123), where all attractions have a roof. The metro station is just steps from the door of BMW Welt.

Beer gardens are off the agenda today (and probably closed) so take your thirst and hunger to a traditional tavern such as the **Hofbräuhaus** (p47) or the **Weisses Bräuhaus** (p50; pictured above).

Get Prepared

BOOK AHEAD

Three months before You will certainly need to book any central accommodation this early as things fill up quickly.

One month before Tickets to any classical music or opera performances need to be booked at least this far in advance.

One week before If you have a plan, tickets to many museums such as the Deutsches Museum can be purchased in advance online.

Manners Matter

Punctuality When meeting up, punctuality is appreciated – never arrive more than 10 minutes late.

Touchy subject It's probably best to avoid conversations about Munich's role in the rise of the Nazis, especially with older people.

At the table Tucking in before the *'Guten Appetit'* starting gun is fired is regarded as bad manners. When drinking wine, the toast is *'Zum Wohl'*, with beer it's *'Prost'*.

Meet the Münchners

Bavarian politeness does not necessarily extend to friendliness and in public, people usually maintain a degree of reserve towards strangers – you won't find many conversations striking up in the supermarket checkout queue. However, in younger company it's easy to chat with just about anyone.

Shaking hands is common among both men and women, as is a hug or a kiss on the cheek, especially among young people.

Things to Know

Supermarkets All supermarkets except those at transport terminals close their doors on Saturday night and reopen on Monday morning.

Reserved Every pub, beer hall and beer garden has a *Stammtisch,* essentially a table reserved for regulars so they don't have to fight for space with tourists in their local pub. If you sit there, staff will move you.

Glass souvenirs Although you pay a deposit for your glass at some beer halls and all beer gardens, it doesn't mean it is yours to keep. Taking it away as a souvenir is theft.

Dress code Smart casual is the attire of choice for upmarket restaurants, the theatre and opera. Shorts or even, heaven forbid, Lederhosen and Dirndl will draw Southern German stares.

TIPPING

It is fine just to round the bill up to the nearest €5 or €10 or not tip at all.

 Restaurants 10%
for very good service

 Bars, pubs, cafes Round up

 Taxis Round up
use app to tip Uber drivers

 Hotel staff Unusual

DAILY BUDGET

BUDGET: Less than €70
- Dorm bed in a hostel: **€32**
- Cheap meal in cafe: **€10–20**
- Museum admission: **€5–8**
- Public-transport day pass: **€9.70**

MIDRANGE: €70–200
- Double en suite room: **€100–150**
- Dinner at a central restaurant: **€50**
- Opera ticket: **€60–100**

TOP END: More than €200
- Upmarket Airbnb or double room in a top-end hotel: from **€250**
- Dinner at a top restaurant: from **€200**
- Private guide per hour: **€25**

Currency
Euro (€)

Languages
German, Bavarian

Time zone
Central European Time (GMT plus one hour)

PANDO HALL/GETTY IMAGES

€1 SUNDAYS

Nine state-run museums charge only a single euro admission on Sundays. This includes several in the Kunstareal and the Bayerisches Nationalmuseum. However, be aware that this rarely includes special and temporary exhibitions.

When To Go

From Advent markets to summer rock festivals and year-round beer bashes – essentially anytime is a good time to come to the Bavarian capital.

Munich is a year-round destination with some festival or folk celebration going on no matter when you turn up. Obviously, in central Europe visitors need to keep one eye on the weather – if subzero temperatures are not your thing, avoid January and February. Munich can also be very muggy in summer. If you are not into beer, the time around Oktoberfest should be avoided. Advent, spring's 'asparagus time', summer's beer garden season and the city's bustling, colourful autumn are some of the best times to visit.

The Big Events

April/May: The first big outdoor bash of the year is the **Frühlingsfest** (Spring Festival), which takes place at several venues across the city with countless beer tents, food stalls and funfair rides.

June/July: Munich's biggest open-air music and culture event is **Tollwood Summer Festival** held at the Olympiapark for four weeks. There's a winter edition on the Theresienwiese during Advent.

September/October: **Oktoberfest** (p134) is the world's largest beer festival and funfair attracting six million visitors over two weeks to its beer tents and rides. Held mostly in September (despite the name) at the Theresienwiese, south of the main train station.

December: For the four weeks leading up to Christmas the **Christkindlmarkt** (p51) takes over the Marienplatz and some nearby streets with bauble stalls and mulled wine.

Munich Weather

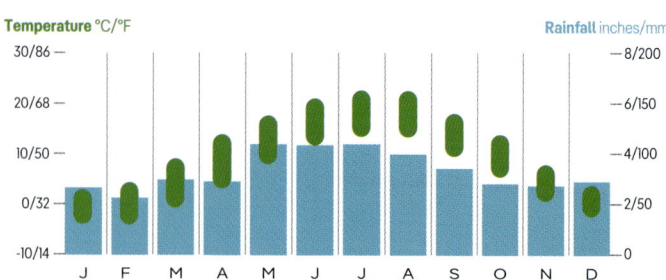

Oktoberfest (p134)

Lesser-known Events

February/March: The 'Time of Strong Beer', aka **Starkbierzeit**, involves some high-percentage lager and is held at various breweries but mainly at the Paulaner am Nockherberg (p113).

June/July: Second only to the Berlin Biennale, the **Munich Film Festival** (Filmfest München) is one of Germany's top film events. It is held at various cinemas through the city.

May/August/October: The **Auer Dult** (Au Fair) is held three times a year on the Mariahilfplatz in Au and involves copious amounts of food and beer as well as a traditional funfair. The October edition comes hot on the heels of Oktoberfest.

October: One of the biggest running events in Germany, the **Munich Marathon** starts and ends at the Olympiapark and takes in many sights in the city centre. There is also a half-marathon race.

ACCOMMODATION LOWDOWN

It is virtually impossible to book a room anywhere in or around Munich during Oktoberfest (late September to early October). There are bargains at weekends and in summer at the Riem Trade Fair Grounds when there are no events taking place.

✈ Getting There

The main point of entry into Munich and all of Bavaria is Munich's Franz Josef Strauss Airport, 27km as the crow flies to the northeast.

From the Airport to the City Centre

S-Bahn
By far the easiest way to get from the airport to downtown Munich is on the S-Bahn light railway network. Munich's airport is linked by the S1 and S8 to the Hauptbahnhof in the centre. The S1 approaches the city centre from the west, the S8 from the east via the Altstadt. The trip costs €14.30, takes about 50 minutes and runs every 10 minutes almost 24 hours a day.

Uber
Uber Airport operates at Munich Airport and a ride to the Altstadt costs around €60. The journey time is around 50 minutes though this can be a lot longer when busy. The pick-up point varies according to the type of vehicle you order and destination.

Bus
The Lufthansa Airport Bus shuttles at 20-minute intervals between the airport and Arnulfstrasse, next to the Hauptbahnhof, between 6.25am and 10.25pm. The trip takes about 45 minutes and costs from €12 (return €19.30).

Other buses leaving from the airport include city buses to Erding and Freising from where there are trains and S-Bahn services into Munich, and Flixbus services to other cities in Germany and beyond.

Other Points of Entry

Zentraler Omnibusbahnhof (ZOB)
The Zentraler Omnibusbahnhof handles the vast majority of international and domestic coach services. There's a Eurolines/Touring office, a supermarket and various eateries on the 1st floor; buses arrive at ground level.

The main operator out of the ZOB is now low-cost coach company Flixbus, which links Munich to countless destinations across Germany and beyond.

Hauptbahnhof (Main Train Station)
Train connections to Munich from destinations in Bavaria are excellent and there are also numerous services from more distant cities within Germany and around Europe. All services pull in at the Hauptbahnhof in the west of the city centre.

Getting Around

Munich has excellent public transport with the S-Bahn, the U-Bahn, trams and buses operated by MVV *(mvv-muenchen.de)* reaching every part of the city. The system is easy to navigate and relatively inexpensive. Other options include a superb network of cycling trails, ride shares and, of course, your own legs, often the best choice in the centre.

S-Bahn

As in most large German cities, the light rail system – the S-Bahn – is the backbone of Munich's public transport system. Lines reach out into the suburbs and beyond. All S-Bahn trains follow the Stammstrecke (central line) through central Munich and services run almost 24 hours a day (approximately 4am to 1am). This is the most convenient mode of transport for getting to/from the airport, Dachau and Oberschleissheim.

U-Bahn

Mostly built for the 1972 Olympics, the modern underground system serves the city centre and the inner suburbs, operating almost 24 hours a day. It's good for medium journeys such as to the Olympiapark and Haidhausen and is much faster than the trams.

Tram

Munich's modern trams (pictured above) link the centre with the inner suburbs and are good for short and medium-length journeys. This is the best way to reach

FROM LEFT: DE-NEU-PIC/SHUTTERSTOCK, ONJIRA LEIBE/SHUTTERSTOCK

— **ESSENTIAL APP** —
The MVV app makes purchasing tickets and planning journeys so much easier.

Nymphenburg and for getting around the city centre without heading underground.

Bus
Munich's extensive network of buses mostly operates in the suburbs, linking residential areas and villages to S-Bahn and U-Bahn stations. Only bus 100, which passes many of the city's museums, is of any use to visitors.

Bike
Munich has one of the best networks of cycle lanes in Europe, which are mostly used by locals to commute to work. Cycle hire is fairly easy to arrange. Bikes can be taken on the S-Bahn but not from 6am to 9am and 4pm to 6pm Monday to Friday (rush hours). All bikes need a ticket. Helmets are not legally required but are of course recommended. Munich's commuters travel very fast along cycle paths – don't dally too much on them.

Ride Share
Uber and other ride-share companies operate in Munich and are normally slightly cheaper than taxis.

Car & Motorcycle
There is little sense in trying to get around Munich with your own wheels. Parking is strictly regulated and pricey, and much of the Altstadt is pedestrianised.

Public Transport Essentials

Buying Tickets
The easiest way to buy tickets is to download the MVV app onto your smartphone, avoiding the need for paper tickets and cash/card transactions. If you do prefer to have a physical ticket, there are ticket machines in every U-Bahn and S-Bahn station and at the railway stations. When using Deutsche Bahn (German Railways) machines, make sure you choose the MVV option.

Fare Zones
Every attraction in this book falls within the M zone – essentially the urban area of Munich – with four exceptions. The airport is in zone M5, Starnberg is in zone M2/3 and the Dachau camp and Oberschleissheim are in zone M1. Maps now show in which zone each station is located. Neuschwanstein is outside the Munich transport system.

Using the System
You must have a ticket before boarding any MVV service. There are no barriers or ticket checkers. You must activate your ticket in the app or stamp paper tickets in machines at stations or in vehicles.

There's no need to show your ticket to bus drivers. Ticket checks by inspectors are common. Those travelling without a ticket, with an inactive or unstamped ticket or in the wrong zone will be fined a minimum of €60.

FOOTOO/SHUTTERSTOCK

TRAVEL COSTS

M1 day travel pass
€9.70

E-scooter per minute
€0.25

Bike rental per day
€20

--- **GROUP SAVING** ---

Zone M Group Day Tickets cost €18.40 and are valid for up to 5 people – exceptional value.

TICKETS
MVV offer myriad tickets but visitors to the city only need to concern themselves with three. These are valid only in the M zone and not for travel to Dachau, the airport, Oberschleissheim or in the unlikely event you are staying outside the Munich urban area.

M Zone Ticket	Cost (€)
Single trip	4.10
Day	9.70
Week	22.40

A Few Surprises

Relics from bygone times, oddities and hidden gems. If you look closely, you'll find some surprising stuff in Munich.

Wild Munich

Many first-time visitors to Munich are surprised what a green and verdant city the Bavarian capital is. In fact, 40% of the city is made up of green spaces, more than any other city in the world! This is helped along significantly by the **Englischer Garten** (p84), one of the planet's largest urban parks at around 15 sq km, but there are many other leafy plots in and around the city centre. Running along the eastern flank of the Englischer Garten is the River Isar, one of the few watercourses in Europe to flow through a major city in its original wild bed. This creates an almost bucolic backdrop to lazy picnics and swimming when the weather is muggy.

Von Gärtner

Leo von Klenze and François de Cuvilliés are the big names of Munich's architectural heritage, having created in brick and plaster the musings of various Wittelsbachs. However, there is a third name, Friedrich von Gärtner (1791–1847), who left an indelible mark on the Bavarian capital. Working under Ludwig I and alongside Klenze, his architectural signature can be found throughout the city centre in the form of the **Ludwigskirche** (p92), the **Feldherrnhalle** (p51), the **Siegestor** (p93), the **main university building** (p88) and the Bayerische Staatsbibliothek – the Bavarian National Library. Von Gärtner is recognised as one of the most important shapers of the Munich cityscape with his own square – or should we say circle – the completely round Gärtnerplatz, just outside the Altstadt.

Afghan Cuisine

Few cities in Europe have such a large Afghan community as Munich. Afghan cuisine consists of

---

OFFBEAT MUNICH

Seek out the tranquil museum where the now-defunct **Ost-West Friedenskirche** (p121) once stood.

Pack your trunks and head to the **Müller'sches Volksbad** (p109), a delightfully olde-worlde Art Nouveau pool.

Wander the time-warped 1972 **Olympic village** (p121) for a journey back to the days of the Economic Miracle.

Make time for the excellent **Sudetendeutsches Museum** (p107) that tells the story of Czechoslovakia's banished German minority.

Englischer Garten (p84)

rice, salads, grilled meats, steamed dumplings, kormas and meat stews, and makes for a delicious dinner. **Chopan** (p133) is one of the standout restaurants.

Famous but Gone!

Munich has several places that have gone down in history but that no longer exist.

Football fans will certainly know about the 1958 Munich air disaster, when a plane carrying the Manchester United team, the Busby Babes, crashed at Munich Airport. However, that wasn't today's airport but Riem Airport, now the trade fair grounds.

Many wrongly assume Hitler launched his Beer Hall Putsch at the Hofbräuhaus but the beer hall in question was the Bürgerbräukeller in Haidhausen, which was demolished in 1979.

One of the most famous buildings in all Munich, the Wittelsbach Palais (where Brienner Strasse and Türkenstrasse meet) witnessed many important events but was torn down in 1964. King Ludwig I retired here in 1848, Ludwig III addressed Munich from the balcony here on the outbreak of WWI, it was the headquarters of the short-lived Bavarian Soviet Republic and it served as a Gestapo jail where the Scholls were imprisoned in 1943.

Explore Munich

Altstadt & the Residenz	35
Maxvorstadt	61
Schwabing & the Englischer Garten	81
Haidhausen, Lehel & Au	101
Nymphenburg, BMW & Olympiapark	115

Worth a Trip

KZ-Gedenkstätte Dachau	78
Schleissheim Palaces	96
Schloss Neuschwanstein	98
Lake Starnberg	138

Munich's Walking Tours

Altstadt	48
Maxvorstadt	72
Schwabing	90
Haidhausen & Au	108
Olympiapark	130

Schloss Nymphenburg (p127)
© BAYERISCHE SCHLÖSSERVERWALTUNG, FLORIAN SCHROTER, WWW.SCHLOESSER.BAYERN.DE

Explore
Altstadt & the Residenz

Centred around the medieval Marienplatz, Munich's central Altstadt is a must-see for all visitors – the neighbourhood contains a couple of top sights as well as the city's best mainstream shopping and a host of eateries.

The Residenz, a sprawling palace from where Bavaria's royals once ruled, should be top of your 'to-visit' list. Combine a trip to the palace with a stroll along Maximilianstrasse, Munich's most exclusive shopping street. For more realistic prices and variety, Kaufingerstrasse and the Stachus are shopping central for locals with flagship stores lining the pedestrianised thoroughfares. Lost amid the retail frenzy on Sendlinger Strasse, the Asamkirche offers up Munich's finest church interior. And when you need to refuel, the Hofbräuhaus and several other traditional taverns are a short stroll away.

Getting Around

 On Foot
As the Altstadt is relatively small and much of it is pedestrianised, walking is the best way to get around.

 Tram
Trams 17, 19 and 21 run through the south of the Altstadt and are a good way of getting from Isartor to Karlsplatz/Stachus without pounding the pavements.

 **Bicycle**
You can cycle everywhere in the Altstadt, but take care on pedestrianised shopping streets such as Kaufingerstrasse and Semdlinger Strasse.

Marienplatz (p42)
NIKADA/GETTY IMAGES

THE BEST

ROYAL OPULENCE Munich Residenz (p38)

EPICENTRAL MEETING POINT Marienplatz (p42)

HOLY SPLENDOUR Asamkirche (p44)

TOP TEMPLE Frauenkirche (p46)

BEST BEER HALL Hofbräuhaus (p47)

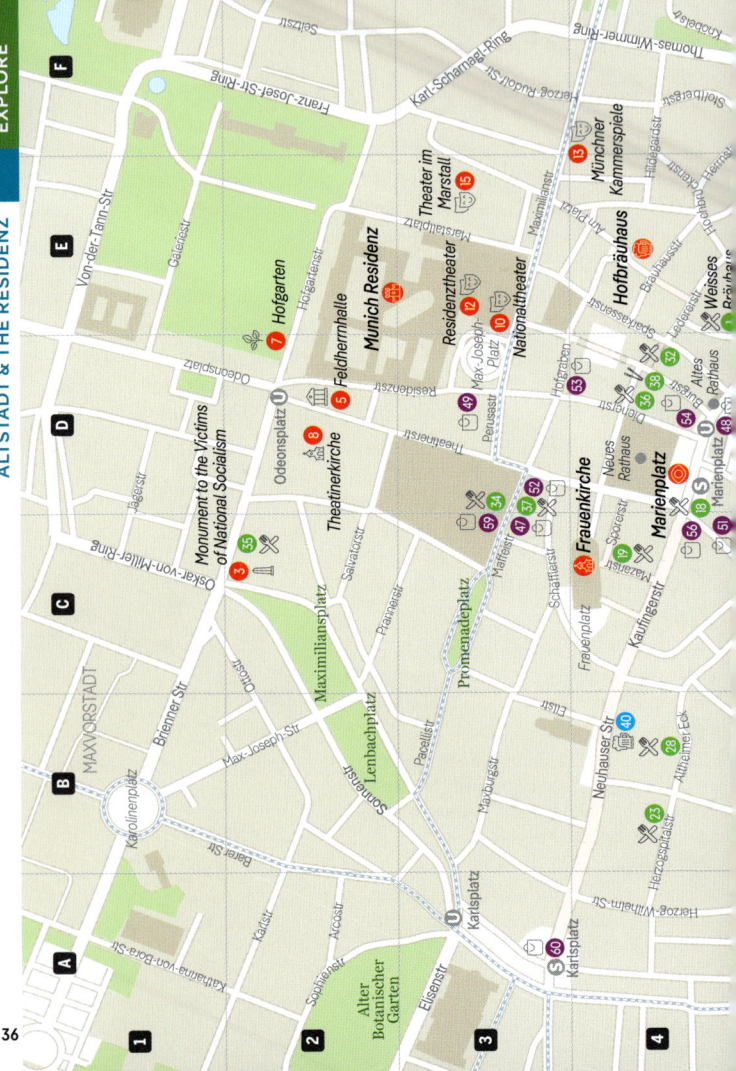

ALTSTADT & THE RESIDENZ

For more see
- Top Experiences p38
- Experiences p50
- Eating p54
- Drinking p56
- Shopping p58

Sights (on map)

- Asamkirche
- Heiliggeistkirche
- Jüdisches Museum
- Münchner Marionettentheater
- Staatstheater am Gärtnerplatz
- Bier & Oktoberfestmuseum
- Viktualienmarkt

0.2 miles / 400 m

★ **TOP EXPERIENCE**

Munich Residenz

Home to Bavaria's all-powerful Wittelsbach rulers from 1508 until WWI, the Residenz is Munich's number one attraction. Taking up a large chunk of the city centre, the palace is one of Europe's largest and includes the baroque Cuvilliés-Theater and the Aladdin's cave that is the *Schatzkammer* (treasury).

MAP P36 **E2**

Ancestors' Gallery, Grottenhof & Antiquarium

The tour of the **Munich Residenz** *(residenz-muenchen.de; ticket for all sights adult/concession €20/16)* kicks off in the rococo **Ahnengallery** (Ancestors Gallery), which showcases 121 portraits of Bavarian rulers in chronological order. All of them played their part in creating the piece of heritage you are about to see, some more than others.

Next comes the **Grottenhof** (Grotto Court), home of the wonderful **Perseusbrunnen** (Perseus Fountain), with its namesake holding the dripping head of Medusa. Look closely and you will see that the decoration here is made entirely of tens of thousands of shells, some huge, some no bigger than a child's fingernail.

Next door is the famous **Antiquarium**, a barrel-vaulted hall of frescos created by Duke Albrecht V between 1568 and 1571 to house the vast royal collection of Greek and Roman sculptures. It is the most impressive and unusual space in Bavaria and claims the title of the largest Renaissance hall north of the Alps. The raised platform at one end enables you to get some incredible shots with a widescreen lens or camera setting.

Living Like a Royal

Generations of big-ego'ed Bavarian royals often shunned their predecessors' living quarters,

PLANNING TIP
For much of the year (not in summer), the Cuvilliés-Theater is only open in the afternoons. Keep your ticket and return later in the day.

Scan for full opening hours and ticket prices.

© BAYERISCHE SCHLÖSSERVERWALTUNG, MARIA SCHERF VERONIA FREUDLING, WWW.SCHLOESSER.BAYERN.DE

preferring instead to commission their own, hence the sheer size and scale of the Residenz complex. Some of the most impressive digs are Cuvilliés' **Kurfürstenzimmer** (Electors Rooms) and the wonderful **Reiche Zimmer**, which live up to their name meaning 'rich'. The **Steine Zimmer** (Stone Rooms) are the finest rococo interiors in southern Germany. Maximilian I's **Kaisersaal** (Imperial Hall), dating from the early 17th century, is a huge space for the time it was built, resplendent in gilt stucco and monster Dutch tapestries. The same ruler also commissioned the impressively stuccoed **Hofkapelle** (Court Chapel), where chamber concerts sometimes take place. In stark contrast to the decorative Hofkapelle, the **All Saints Church** has unrendered brick walls, with restorers having left the structure partially as it was after WWII.

QUICK BREAK
Schumanns Tagesbar (p56), a block away from the Residenz in Maffeistrasse, is a madly popular lunch, coffee or Aperol spot and the ideal place to wait for the Cuvilliés-Theater to open.

MUNICH RESIDENZ
Ground floor

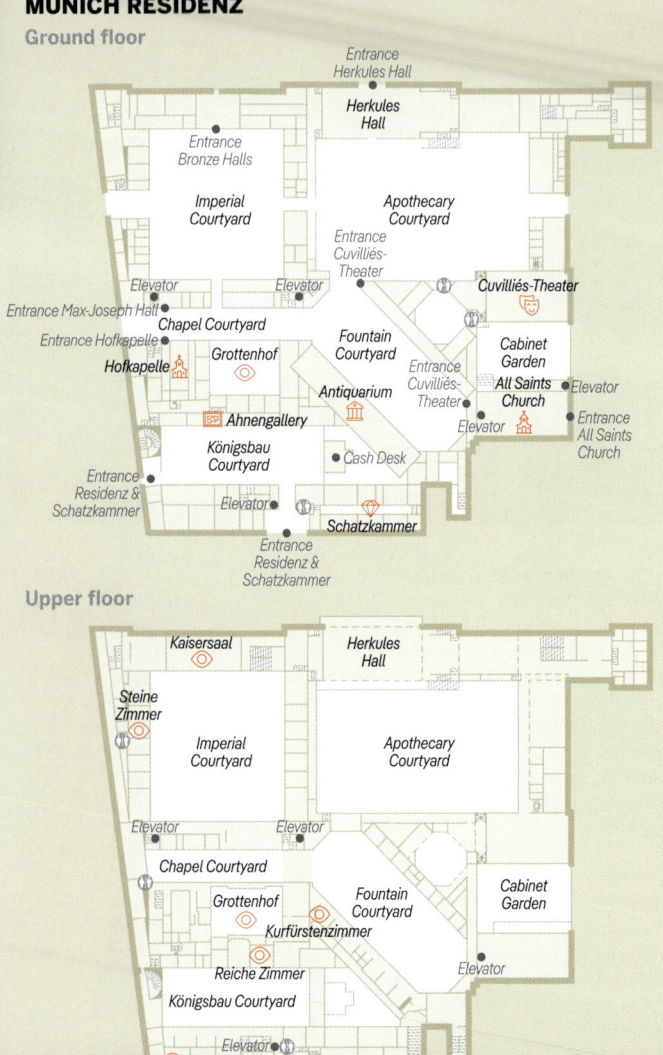

Upper floor

Ludwig I's Royal Palace

The cherry on the Wittelsbach cake and the climax of their over-the-top grandeur comes in the form of Ludwig I's **Royal Palace**. This no-holds-barred series of neoclassical quarters includes the king's throne room with its entirely gold walls, Roman stucco and huge red-velvet canopy. Sadly, everything you see here is a complete rebuild as this part of the Residenz was reduced to neo-Renaissance landfill in 1944.

Schatzkammer

After your tour of the main palace, the **Schatzkammer der Residenz** contains the Wittelsbachs' collections of jewel-encrusted yesteryear bling. The low-lit space highlights the sheer magnificence of the priceless objects they amassed, which are dramatically illuminated in show cabinets. Highlights include the Bavarian crown insignia, the delicate Gothic crown of Anne of Bohemia (the oldest English crown in existence) and ruby-and-diamond-encrusted jewellery of Queen Therese (1792–1854). It takes no more than 40 minutes to get round the well-curated exhibition.

Cuvilliés-Theater

As it is usually closed until around 2pm, most visitors come back later in the day to visit the wonderfully maintained baroque **Cuvilliés-Theater**, the Wittelsbachs' little piece of home entertainment. Take a seat and lift your gaze to the four levels of balconies, each one plastered in gilt and red stucco. Illuminated with candles (albeit today with electronic versions for obvious reasons), it's easy to imagine what a magical experience a performance here in the mid-18th century would have been. Cuvilliés' creation is famous for hosting the premiere of Mozart's opera *Idomeneo* and performances still take place here occasionally. Access is limited to the auditorium.

FRANÇOIS DE CUVILLIÉS

Belgium-born François de Cuvilliés (1695–1768) is the architect who had the greatest influence on the appearance of the Wittelsbachs' Munich residence. He was appointed court architect in 1724 by Maximilian II but worked under Charles VII and Maximilian III, for whom he created the baroque theatre that now bears his name. Another of his masterpieces is the Amalienburg at Schloss Nymphenburg (p127).

★ TOP EXPERIENCE

Marienplatz

Munich's epicentral heart and soul, Marienplatz is essential viewing for any visitor, most of whom find themselves here at some point. It's a popular gathering spot and Munich's busiest piazza by far, with throngs of tourists swarming across its expanse from early morning until late at night.

MAP P36 **D4**

PLANNING TIP

The Glockenspiel on the Neues Rathaus springs into action every day at 11am and noon, as well as at 5pm from March to October.

Scan for full opening hours and more information on the Neues Rathaus.

Neues Rathaus

Apart from the 1638 **Mariensäule** (St Mary's Column) and the 1950s **Fischbrunnen** (Fish Fountain; pictured right) on the eastern side, the inventory of the square is limited. However, there always seems to be something going on here, from political rallies to spring asparagus markets. This is the main venue for Munich's **Christmas markets**.

The real interest is in what surrounds the square. Completely dominating the northern flank, the soot-blackened facade of the neogothic **Neues Rathaus** (*New City Hall; tower adult/child €7/3*) is festooned with gargoyles, statues and a turret-scaling dragon; the city's main tourist office is on the ground floor. For pinpointing Munich's landmarks without losing your breath, take the lift up the 85m-tall tower. Back on the ground, look up to watch the **Glockenspiel** with its 43 bells and 32 figures that perform two historical events. The top half tells the story of a tournament held in 1568 to celebrate the marriage of Duke Wilhelm V to Renata of Lothringen, while the bottom half portrays the *Schäfflertanz* (coopers' dance). The Glockenspiel performs twice a day, with the whole performance taking between 12 and 15 minutes, depending on which tune is played.

The Neues Rathaus is the next major building in Munich set for renovation, which could last years.

OLHA SOLODENKO/SHUTTERSTOCK

Altes Rathaus

On the Marienplatz' eastern flank you'll find the **Altes Rathaus**. Lightning got the better of the medieval original in 1460 and WWII bombs levelled its successor, so what you see is really the third incarnation of the building designed by Jörg von Halspach of Frauenkirche fame. On 9 November 1938, Joseph Goebbels gave a hate-filled speech here that launched the nationwide Kristallnacht pogroms.

St Peterskirche

Just off the southern side of the Marienplatz rises the impressive 1150 **St Peterskirche**. The highlight is the tower – 306 steps take you to the best view of central Munich. Inside are the Gothic St-Martin-Altar, the baroque ceiling fresco by Johann Baptist Zimmermann and rococo sculptures by Ignaz Günther.

QUICK BREAK
The obvious place to head for a bite to eat when visiting the Marienplatz is the adjacent **Viktualienmarkt** (p53) for picnic supplies or lunch on the go.

★ TOP EXPERIENCE

Asamkirche

Rising unexpectedly amid the modern facades of Sendlinger Strasse and largely ignored by scurrying shoppers, the pocket-sized, late-baroque Asamkirche, built in 1746, is as rich and epic as a giant's treasure chest, with every inch of wall space decorated in the way only the counter-Reformation knew how.

MAP P36 **B5**

Facade
Before entering the church, stop for a moment to look at the frontage, a typical piece of high baroque wedged between later facades. Notice how the architects made it look as though the building is clamped to the bedrock, a common feature with churches dedicated to St Nepomuk. However, the rock is artificial (it doesn't continue on the inside): a typical bit of counter-Reformation illusion. To the right of the church is the house which Egid Quirin Asam bought in the 18th century, still a splendid sight with its figurative stucco facade.

PLANNING TIP
The Asamkirche is normally closed on Friday mornings and for services. It's free to enter.

Baroque Glory
The Asamkirche is primarily the work of Egid Quirin Asam, though he had a little help from his brother, Cosmas Damian Asam. It was originally designed as their private chapel which they could access directly from their quarters next door.

On entering the church, small by central Europe's monumental baroque standards, the nave is a dazzling, almost overwhelming spectacle with no surface left unadorned. Faux marble gleams in every shade possible, stucco curtains are draped over the balcony in the upper levels and four extra-large barley twist columns adorn the altar, behind which explodes a gilt baroque

Scan for full opening hours and for more details on the history of the Asamkirche.

EO/SHUTTERSTOCK

sunburst. Grab yourself a pew and try to take it all in.

When you are done with the walls, the crowning glory is the ceiling fresco illustrating the life of St John Nepomuk, to whom the church is dedicated (lie down on your back in a pew to fully appreciate the complicated perspective). This was the work of Cosmas Damian.

Final Resting Place

Egid Quirin Asam is actually buried in the crypt of the church, below his *'Liabe Kircherl'* ('beloved church' in Bavarian dialect). Sadly, when he died in 1750, the church was not entirely finished. The space containing his tomb has fallen into disrepair and there is a fundraising effort to have it restored and opened to the public.

QUICK BREAK
Just around the corner from the Asamkirche, in Hackenstrasse, is **Prinz Myshkin** (p55), one of Munich's best vegetarian restaurants, with an imaginative menu and a bright dining space.

★ TOP EXPERIENCE

Frauenkirche

The Altstadt has several churches, but the top temple in all Munich is the Frauenkirche, an instantly recognisable symbol on the city's skyline. And why do its twin, onion-dome-topped towers still dominate? Well, the rule is that no building in the Altstadt can stand taller than its 99m.

MAP P36 **C4**

The Interior

The Frauenkirche was built between 1468 and 1488, but was severely damaged during WWII. The rebuild created a rather spartan interior, with a low-lit shaft of tall whitewashed columns. Side chapels behind tall iron railings are dedicated to various saints and guilds and some of the church's impossibly elongated windows disappear up into the haze in a riot of stained glass. The crypt is a strangely modern affair containing the **tomb of Ludwig the Bavarian**. The nave is free to enter.

Another notable buried in a chapel beneath the north tower is Jörg von Halsbach, the local architect who built the Frauenkirche.

Climbing the Tower

The highlight (though a rather pricey one) for most visitors here is the opportunity to climb the **south tower** *(adult/child €7.50/5.50)* which measures 98.45m, 12cm shorter than the north tower. A modern lift takes you to the top from where you can peer out of the small windows across the whole of Munich. It's clear from up here that the height rule for new buildings in the Altstadt at least is adhered to with southern German thoroughness. You can also admire the architectural detail of the north tower rising close by.

PLANNING TIP
Organ concerts take place every Wednesday evening in July and August. Tickets can be purchased from the cathedral shop on the day.

Scan for full opening hours and ticket prices at the Frauenkirche.

★ TOP EXPERIENCE

Hofbräuhaus

Even committed teetotallers should at least poke their heads around the door of the Hofbräuhaus, Munich institution and the world's most celebrated beer hall. For those into Central European lager, a night on the Hofbräu is like the culmination of a hop-scented pilgrimage.

MAP P36 **E4**

A Little History

Arguably the world's best-known beer hall, Munich's illustrious **Hofbräuhaus** *(hofbraeuhaus.de)* was founded in 1589 by Duke Wilhelm V to supply the royal court with decent lager, hence the name of the beer here – Hofbräu – which means 'court brew'. The beer hall had gone public by the 1830s, transforming into one of Munich's most popular drinking and meeting spots. Seriously damaged during WWII, it was quickly rebuilt and has attracted thirsty locals and tourists ever since.

The HB Experience

The Hofbräuhaus is a beer hall and tourist attraction rolled into one: take a seat in the main hall or in the horse-chestnut-shaded garden, order a *Mass* (1L tankard) and some Bavarian food and sway with the other tourists to the oompah band. Within this wondrously cavernous pub, you'll discover a range of spaces in which to do your elbow bending: the garden, the main hall next to the oompah band, tables opposite the industrial-scale kitchen and quieter corners. One interesting feature is that you must buy your beer with prepaid beer tokens, just like during Oktoberfest. Buy 10 tokens (equal to 10 litres of lager) and the eleventh is free. There's also an interesting gift shop on the premises.

PLANNING TIP
The Hofbräuhaus splits at the seams on weekend evenings though it is also at its most raucously atmospheric. Go during the week or at lunchtime if you prefer a quieter experience.

Scan for more on the Hofbräuhaus.

WALKING TOUR

Walk the Altstadt

Munich's Altstadt is quite a place of contrasts, from always-busy squares to peaceful courtyards, raucous beer halls to forgotten pieces of parkland, obscure monuments to luxury retail. This walk takes you across the Altstadt's widest diameter, with plenty of places to stop for refreshments along the way.

START	END	LENGTH
Karlsplatz/Stachus	Hofbräuhaus	1.6km; one hour

1 Busy Square

Karlsplatz and the medieval Karlstor (a gate) form the western entrance to the Altstadt and the pedestrianised shopping precinct along Neuhauser Strasse and Kaufinger Strasse. The busy square was laid out in 1791 as an egocentric project of the highly unpopular Elector Karl Theodor. Busy above and below ground, locals call the area the **Stachus** after a pub that once stood here.

2 Beer Temple

Right in the thick of the retail frenzy on Neuhauser Strasse is the humungous **Augustiner Stammhaus** (p56) belonging to the Augustiner Brewery. Out back is a peaceful, ancient arcaded beer garden.

3 Tomb of the 'Mad King'

It stands quiet and dignified amid the retail frenzy out on Kaufingerstrasse, but to fans of Ludwig II, the **Michaelskirche** is a place of pilgrimage. Its dank crypt is the final resting place of the 'Mad King', whose surprisingly humble tomb is usually buried in flowers.

4 Michael Jackson Shrine

What do the late Renaissance composer Orlando di Lasso and Michael Jackson have in common? Nothing, apart from the fact that Jackson fans chose the obscure 16th-century music-maker's monument to create a photo- and memorabilia-bedecked shrine to their idol when he passed away in 2009. Jackson used to stay at the Hotel Bayerischer Hof nearby.

5 Shopping Street

In the market for a Rolex, a Gucci handbag, a little piece of Cartier or a luxury classic car? Well, **Maximilianstrasse** can provide them all, as this is Munich's most affluent shopping street… or should that be window-shopping street?

6 Home of the Opera

The Bavarian State Opera performs to sell-out crowds at the **Bayerisches Nationaltheater**, which also hosts Munich's top opera event, the Opernfestspiele. The opera's house band is the Bayerisches Staatsorchester, in business since 1523.

7 Wittelsbachs' Palace

Alter Hof was the starter home of the Wittelsbach family and has its origins in the 12th century. The Bavarian rulers moved out of this central palace as long ago as the 15th century. Visitors can only see the central courtyard where there's a special tourist office dedicated to the castles of Bavaria.

8 World-famous Beer Hall

If you've worked up a thirst, you are at the doors of the **Hofbräuhaus** (p47), where the Hofbräu brewery's creations are downed nightly by locals and tourists alike. Push open the doors and join them. *Prost!*

EXPERIENCES

Have the Weisswurst Experience
LOCAL FOOD

MAP: ① P36 **E4**

A must-have foodie experience when in the Bavarian capital is a *Weisswurst* breakfast at the Altstadt's **Weisses Bräuhaus** *(weisses-brauhaus-tal.de)*. Downing a pair of white veal sausages, a fresh pretzel and a mug of wheat beer at 9am is an essential Munich experience and nowhere does it better. In line with tradition, the tavern only serves *Weisswurst* until noon on the dot. When the bells of the Altstadt chime midday, any Münchner worth their *wurst* will push a plate of them away, declaring them unfresh.

Explore Munich's Jewish Past
JEWISH HERITAGE

MAP: ② P36 **C5**

Coming to terms with its Nazi past has not historically been a priority in Munich, which is why the opening of the **Jüdisches Museum** *(juedisches-museum-muenchen.de; adult/child €6/3)* just over two decades ago was hailed as a real milestone. The permanent exhibition entitled 'Voices_Places_Times' offers an insight into Jewish history, life, rituals and culture in the city, with the last section using comic strips to bridge the gap between the past and present.

Remember the Victims
MONUMENT

MAP: ③ P36 **C2**

The striking **Monument to the Victims of National Socialism** is made up of four Ts holding up a block-like cage in which an eternal flame gutters in remembrance of those who died at the hands of the Nazis due to their political beliefs, race, religion, sexual orientation or disability. Moved to this spot in 2014, it's a sternly simple reminder of Munich's not-so-distant past.

Learn the Story of Oktoberfest
MUSEUM

MAP: ④ P36 **E5**

Head to the popular **Bier & Oktoberfestmuseum** *(bier-und-oktoberfestmuseum.de; adult/concession €4/2.50)* to learn all about Bavarian

---

 WEISSWURST 101

So what exactly is *Weisswurst*? Traditionally these thick, 12cm-long sausages are made from minced veal and pork fat and flavoured with parsley, lemon, mace, onions, ginger and cardamon. When served in the proper traditional way, a pair of them come with a dollop of sweet, runny, grainy mustard, a freshly baked pretzel and, of course, a large mug of wheat beer (*Weissbier*, to go with the *Weisswurst*). They are only eaten until noon, after which they are deemed 'unfresh'.

---  **CHRISTKINDLMARKT** ---

Munich's popular Christmas market is held every year throughout Advent on Marienplatz and the adjoining Rindermarkt. Although not as illustrious as more sparkly Yuletide bazaars in Nuremberg and Dresden, the Munich Christkindlmarkt has been running since 1972, and against the backdrop of the Neues Rathaus can still be a magically atmospheric affair. Locals and visitors gather round the huge Christmas tree as seasonal music rings out from the town hall's balcony. Almost 140 stalls pack the two squares and the streets in between selling the inevitable *Glühwein* (mulled wine), lots of traditional food and countless baubles and trinkets.

---

suds and the world's most famous booze-up. The four floors heave with old brewing vats, historic photos and some of the earliest Oktoberfest regalia. The 14th-century building has some fine medieval features, including painted ceilings and a kitchen with an open fire. If during your tour you've worked up a thirst, the museum has its very own pub.

Feel History at the Feldherrnhalle

MONUMENT

MAP: 5 P36 D2

Corking up Odeonsplatz' southern side is Friedrich von Gärnter's **Feldherrnhalle**, modelled on the Loggia dei Lanzi in Florence. The structure pays homage to the Bavarian army and includes statues of General Johann Tilly, who kicked the Swedes out of Munich during the Thirty Years' War.

General Johann Tilly statue, Feldherrnhalle

MUNICH PRIDE

The city's **Pride Weeks** (csdmuenchen.de) in May and June are by far Munich's biggest LGBTIQ+ events. Things kick off with myriad exhibitions, parties and demonstrations. These run until the third weekend in June and culminate in the main Munich Pride (Christopher Street Day), which was attended in 2025 by well over half a million people, making it one of the largest annual happenings in the city. One of the biggest parties during Pride Weeks is the Glockenbach street festival, one of the oldest street festivals in the Bavarian capital.

It was here on 9 November 1923 that police stopped the so-called Beer Hall Putsch, Hitler's attempt to bring down the Weimar Republic (Germany's government after WWI). A fierce skirmish left 20 people, including 16 Nazis, dead. A plaque in the pavement on the square's eastern side commemorates the police officers who perished in the incident.

All Hail the Heiliggeistkirche
CHURCH

MAP: ❻ P36 **D5**

Gothic at its core, the baroque **Heiliggeistkirche** on the edge of the Viktualienmarkt has fantastic ceiling frescos created by the Asam brothers in 1720, depicting the foundation of a hospice that once stood next door. The hospice was demolished to make way for the new Viktualienmarkt.

Picnic in the Hofgarten
PARK

MAP: ❼ P36 **D2**

Office workers catching some rays during their lunch break, stylish mothers pushing prams, seniors on bikes, a gaggle of chatty nuns – everybody comes to the **Hofgarten**. The formal former court gardens, with fountains, radiant flowerbeds, lime-tree-lined gravel paths and benches galore, sit just north of the Residenz. Paths converge at the Dianatempel, a striking octagonal pavilion honouring the Roman goddess of the hunt. The Hofgarten is one of the best places for a city-centre supermarket picnic, though bench space in the shade can come at a premium. Enter the gardens from Odeonsplatz.

Descend to the Royal Crypt
CHURCH

MAP: ❽ P36 **D2**

The mustard-yellow **Theatinerkirche**, built to commemorate the 1662 birth of Prince Max Emanuel, is the work of Swiss architect Enrico Zuccalli. Also known as St Kajetan's, it's a voluptuous design with massive twin towers flanking a giant cupola. Inside, an ornate dome lords it over the *Fürstengruft* (royal crypt), the final destination of several Wittelsbach rulers, including King Maximilian II (1811–64).

Shop for Gourmet Supplies at the Viktualienmarkt
MARKET

MAP: ⑨ P36 **D5**

Looking for a tub of gourmet olives, some Brazilian mangoes, bio *Weisswurst,* a wedge of Alpine cheese, a *maracuja* (passion fruit) smoothie bucket or some pickled, well, anything? Just steps from the Marienplatz is Munich's most famous market, the open-air **Viktualienmarkt** *(viktualienmarkt-muenchen.de).* Originally the city's fruit and veg market, it's been here for more than 200 years and occupies 18,000 sq metres of prime city-centre real estate.

However, this is no ordinary farmers market. Over the past two decades the Viktualienmarkt has become a dining hot spot, with countless stalls offering tasty gourmet (and not so gourmet) snacks.

BEST CULTURE HOTSPOTS
The Altstadt is home to many of Munich's top cultural institutions.

Nationaltheater
MAP: ⑩ P36 **E3**
Home to the world-class Bavarian State Opera.

Staatstheater am Gärtnerplatz
MAP: ⑪ P36 **D7**
This grand theatre specialises in light opera, musicals and dance.

Residenztheater
MAP: ⑫ P36 **E3**
The Bayerisches Staatsschauspiel performs here.

Münchner Kammerspiele
MAP: ⑬ P36 **F4**
Classic plays and new works performed at an Art Nouveau theatre and in a 21st-century glass cube, the Neues Haus.

Münchner Marionettentheater
MAP: ⑭ P36 **B7**
The city's puppet theatre, located on Blumenstrasse.

Theater im Marstall
MAP: ⑮ P36 **E3**
Also a venue for the Bayerisches Staatsschauspiel theatre ensemble.

LISTINGS

Best Places for...

☕ Budget ☕☕ Midrange ☕☕☕ Top End

Eating

Coffee & Kuchen

Götterspeise ☕
16 B8

The name of this cafe translates as 'food of the gods' and the food in question is that most addictive of treats, chocolate. Here it comes in many forms, both liquid and solid, but there are also teas, coffees and cakes. *8am-7pm Mon-Fri, to 6pm Sat*

Schmalznudel ☕
17 C5

This incredibly popular institution serves just four traditional pastries, one of which, the *Schmalznudel* (an oily type of doughnut), gives the place its local nickname. All baked goodies you munch here are crisp and fragrant. *8am-6pm Mon-Sat*

Café Glockenspiel ☕
18 D4

This cafe just off Marienplatz is a touristy affair, but has excellent views across Munich's main square and of City Hall. Gets busy with tourists seeking caffeine. *9am-11pm Mon-Sat, 10am-6.30pm Sun*

True Bavarian

Augustiner Stammhaus ☕☕
see B4

Monster beer hall on a major pedestrianised shopping street with a number of different halls and rooms, a tranquil, old-world courtyard and hearty Bavarian food and lager. *10am-midnight*

Andechser am Dom ☕☕
19 C4

If you want to taste the the monastery-brewed Andechs without the trip out to Andechs itself, head for this stylish tavern opposite the Frauenkirche. The traditional Bavarian food is almost as good as the beer. *11am-midnight*

Fraunhofer ☕☕
20 C7

With its screechy parquet floors, stuccoed ceilings, wood panelling and virtually no trace that the last century even happened, this wonderfully characterful inn is perfect for exploring the region with a fork. *5pm-1am*

Weisses Bräuhaus ☕☕
see E4

One of Munich's classic beer halls, with Alpine whoops accompanying the rabble-rousing oompah band. Specialises in wheat beer and the *Weisswurst* breakfast. *9am-10pm*

Bratwurstherzl ☕☕
21 D5

Cosy panelling and an ancient vaulted brick ceiling set the tone of this Old Munich tavern with a Franconian focus. Homemade organic sausages are grilled to perfection on an open beechwood fire. *10am-11pm Mon-Sat*

Zum Dürnbräu ☕☕
22 E5

This wood-panelled and hunting trophy–bedecked

tavern flies somewhat under the radar and offers excellent Bavarian food and beer in a quieter ambience than some of its bigger-name competitors. *11am-11pm Mon-Sat*

Weinhaus Neuner €€€
 B4

This Munich institution has been serving Bavarian-Austrian classics and a long wine list for well over 100 years. Take a break from the hops-infused frenzy to enjoy schnitzel and *Tafelspitz* (boiled veal or beef), helped along with a Franconian Riesling or a Wachau Grüner Veltiner. *noon-midnight Mon-Sat*

Vegan & Vegetarian

Die Vegane Fleischerei €
㉔ D5

The 'Vegan Butchery' has a wide range of mock meats, cheeses and other dishes, plus lunchtime soups and light meals that can be enjoyed on a few tables. There is also takeaway. *11.30am-8pm Mon-Sat*

Prinz Myshkin €€
㉕ B5

Ensconced in a former brewery, Munich's premier meat-free dining spot occupies a gleamingly whitewashed, vaulted space where health-conscious eaters come to savour imaginative plant-based dishes and 'wellness desserts'. *11am-11pm Tue-Sat*

Secret Garden €€
㉖ D5

Tucked behind the Heiliggeistkirche, this vegan sushi and Asian fusion restaurant is arguably the best plant-based feeding spot in the Altstadt. The lunch menu is good value. *noon-11pm*

Non-Bavarian Eats

Ruff's Burger €
 C5

In a strategic spot on the Rindermarkt that catches many people coming off the Marienplatz, this branch of Ruff's is ideal if all you want to do is quickly satisfy your pangs with a tasty patty. *11am-9pm*

NIGIN €€
㉘ B4

Munich has such a large Afghan population that the local Afghan dining scene is well worth checking out, especially if you've never 'gone Afghan'. Expect lots of rice, salads, roast meats and a complete absence of alcohol at this colourful place. *noon-midnight*

Hewad €€
 B6

Great little Afghan dinner place in the south of the Altstadt serving salads, spicy rice dishes and grilled meats. No alcohol. *5-11pm*

Indian Love Story €€
㉚ E5

Arguably the most authentic Indian dining experience in the Altstadt, with lots of spicy street food, vegan and vegetarian options and friendly staff. *11.30am-2.30pm & 5.30-11.30pm Mon-Fri, noon-11pm Sat & Sun*

Einstein €€€
 C5

Reflected in the plate-glass windows of the Jüdisches Museum, this is the only kosher eatery in the city centre. The ID-and-bag-search entry process is worth it for the restaurant's uncluttered lines, smartly laid tables, soothing ambience and menu of well-crafted kosher dishes. *noon-2.30pm & 6-10.30pm Mon-Wed, 12.30-2.30pm Fri*

Galleria €€€
㉜ D4

Munich has a multitude of Italian eateries, but Galleria is a cut above the rest. The compact interior hits you first, a multihued, eclectic mix of contemporary art and tightly packed tables. The menu contains a few non-Italian surprises. *noon-2.30pm & 6.30-11pm*

Brunch & Lunch

Münchner Suppenküche €
33 C5

If all you fancy is a bowl of soup, this small, welcoming place always has around five on the go, plus fruit salads and coffees. *10am-4pm Mon-Fri*

Schumanns Tagesbar €€
34 D3

Near the Residenz, this simply stylish bistro-bar is packed to the gills at lunchtime as it serves some of the best light meals in the Altstadt. It then doubles up as an early-closing bar later in the day. *8am-9pm Mon-Fri, to 7pm Sat*

Cafe Luitpold €€
35 C2

Around for as long as anyone can remember, this is good for a daytime coffee-and-cake stop, a light lunch or a full evening blowout with all the trimmings. Breakfast served until 3pm. *8am-10pm Mon-Sat, 9am-8pm Sun*

Fine Dining

Alois – Dallmayr Fine Dining €€€
36 D4

Enjoy the double Michelin–starred food menu by head chef Rosina Ostler at this top-drawer Munich stalwart. *12.30-3pm Thu-Sat, 7pm-midnight Wed-Sat*

Les Deux €€€
37 D3

The modern French cuisine at this restaurant near the Frauenkirche has earned it a Michelin twinkler. Book well ahead. *noon-midnight Mon-Sat*

Tohru €€€
38 D4

Minimalist Michelin Japanese cuisine in a retro-styled dining room prepared by Munich-born chef of German-Japanese descent, Tohru Nakamura. *7pm-midnight Tue-Sat*

Le Stollberg €€€
39 F5

Intimate little restaurant serving Bavarian food with Mediterranean touches crafted by owner-chef Anette Huber. *11.30am-2.30pm & 6pm-midnight Wed-Fri, 4.30-11pm Sat*

Drinking

Beer Halls

Augustiner Stammhaus
40 B4

This sprawling place has a less raucous atmosphere and superior food to the usual offerings. Altogether it's a much more authentic example of an old-style Munich beer hall, but with the added highlight of a tranquil arcaded beer garden out back. *11am-late*

Tegernseer Tal
41 D5

A blond-wood interior illuminated by a huge skylight makes this a bright alternative to Munich's dark-panelled taverns. And with Alpine Tegernseer beer on tap and an imaginative menu of regional food, this is generally a lighter, calmer, more refined beer-hall experience with a less boisterous ambience. *9.30am-1am Sun-Wed, to 3am Thu-Sat*

Der Pschorr
42 D5

Flagship restaurant of the Hacker-Pschorr brewery at the Viktualienmarkt, known as much for its excellent food as it is for the lager. The high-ceilinged interior with its wood panelling is packed out every night of the year. *11am-11pm*

Beer Gardens

Viktualienmarkt
see D5

The most central of Munich's beer gardens is at the Viktualienmarkt. Here, Munich's big six breweries take turns to pump lager to thirsty diners and shoppers. You can wait a while for a table on sunny days. *10am-10pm Mon-Sat*

Braunauer Hof
 E5

Near the Isartor, drinkers can choose between the traditional Bavarian interior or the beer garden out the back, which enjoys a surprisingly tranquil setting despite its city-centre location. Most come for the Paulaner beer in the evening. *11am-11.30pm Mon-Sat*

Cool Cafes

Cafe Pini
 C7

Italian cafe that recalls the days of the Economic Miracle when Italian *Gastarbeiter* (foreign workers) streamed into Munich. The retro interior comes as a pleasant surprise, as do the superb espressos and paninis. *9am-11pm Mon-Sat, to 7pm Sun*

Baader Café
 D8

Eclectic cafe serving coffee by day and cocktails by night to a very mixed crowd. The excellent attempt at a full English breakfast will be appreciated by many of the Anglo-Saxon persuasion. *10am-1am*

Trachtenvogl
 D8

At night you'll have to shoehorn your way into this buzzy lair favoured by a chatty crowd of cool locals. Daytimes are more mellow – all the better to sample the seasonal menu and check out the collection of knick-knacks left over from the days when this was a traditional clothes shop. *9am-10pm*

Alois – Dallmayr Fine Dining

Shopping

Trachten & Dirndl

Loden-Frey
47 C3

For a better-standard, keep-forever, upmarket Lederhosen and Dirndl outfit head to this high-priced shop with a tradition going back to 1842. *10am-8pm Mon-Sat*

Inntaler Trachtenwelt
48 D4

Just off the Marienplatz, this supplier has traditional garb for men, women and children. *10am-8pm Mon-Sat*

Gössl
49 D3

The Munich branch of an Austrian traditional alpine clothing seller has a wide variety of colourfully understated traditional dresses that are a joy to own. *10am-6.30pm Mon-Sat*

Sports & Outdoors

Globetrotter
50 E5

Munich's premier outdoors and travel stockist is worth a browse even if you've never pulled on a pair of hiking boots. As well as every travel and outdoor accessory you could ever possibly need, the store even boasts a lake for testing out kayaks. *10am-7pm Mon-Sat*

Schuster
51 C4

Get tooled up for the Alps at this sports megastore boasting seven shiny floors of equipment, including cycling, skiing, travel and camping paraphernalia. *10am-8pm Mon-Sat*

FC Bayern World
52 D3

Bayern Munich's flagship merch store just off the Marienplatz selling everything from wildly overpriced team shirts to keyrings and ties. There are several others in Munich and across Bavaria. *10am-8pm Mon-Sat*

Homewares & Department Stores

Manufactum
53 D4

Anyone with an admiration for top-quality design from Germany and further afield should make a beeline for this store. Last-a-lifetime household items compete for shelf space with retro toys, Bauhaus lamps and times-gone-by stationery. *9.30am-7pm Mon-Sat*

Ludwig Beck
54 D4

Just sneaking onto the Marienplatz, the Ludwig Beck department store is a retail experience of the highest quality with prices to match. Good for a wander even if you don't want to buy. *10am-8pm Mon-Sat*

Kustermann
55 D5

For over 220 years this upmarket department store has been supplying homewares to Munich's upper-middle classes. Whatever you buy here, it will be the last word in solid design and quality. *10am-7pm Mon-Sat*

Galeria Kaufhof Marienplatz
56 C4

Right on the Marienplatz, when you are done perusing the myriad wares this department store stocks, head for the 5th-floor restaurant that has distracting views of the Neues Rathaus. *10am-8pm Mon-Sat*

Bottles & Glashaus
57 B5

If it's made of glass, this wonderfully stocked

backstreet shop sells it, from jam jars to wine glasses, marbles to vases, paperweights to Venetian-style beads. *noon-6pm Mon-Fri*

Food & Drink
Viktualienmarkt
see D5

Munich's central market is the best place in the Altstadt to grab a sausage in a bun, source some gourmet pickles or hang out with a glass of Austrian wine. Prices aren't the lowest but most of what is sold here is top quality. *8am-8pm Mon-Sat*

Schrannenhalle
58 D5

The old indoor food market is now an Italian speciality megamarket with every ingredient you could possibly imagine from the *bel paese* weighing down shelves. There are tasting sessions and events as well as a cafe. *9am-10pm Mon-Sat*

Arcades & Malls
Fünf Höfe
59 C3

This large shopping mall is concealed behind numerous facades to the west of the Residenz. As well as the numerous mainstream and flagship stores here, there's a handy supermarket in the basement for on-the-go snacks. *10am-8pm Mon-Sat*

Stachus Passagen
60 A3

This huge, modern shopping mall lurks beneath Karlsplatz and has direct access to the U-Bahn station. The more than 60 businesses based here include many handy bakeries and fast-food joints. *10am-7pm Mon-Sat*

Preloved Clothing
Capricorn Store
61 D8

Design-concept preloved women's clothing boutique in the fashionable Gärtnerplatzviertel south of the Altstadt where pieces are painstakingly selected and sold on to appreciating clients. *11am-7pm Mon-Fri, to 6pm Sat*

Picknweight
 E5

The Altstadt branch of this popular secondhand vintage-clothing chain is an Aladdin's cave of denim and leather, flowery dresses and colourful shirts. You pay according to how much the clothes weigh. *11am-8pm Mon-Sat*

See p76 for eating, drinking and shopping listings

Explore
Maxvorstadt

To the northwest of the Altstadt, Maxvorstadt is home to the Kunstareal, or Art Quarter, a whole neighbourhood dedicated to museums and art galleries. Gathered around Ludwig I's Athens-esque Königsplatz and in the parks between Arcistrasse and Türkenstrasse, in no other area of southern Germany (or perhaps even central Europe) will you encounter such a high concentration of art. The Pinakotheken, the Museum Brandhorst and various other institutions both old and new come together in one of Munich's must-sees, enjoyable even if you can't yet tell a Rembrandt from a Renoir.

Another, darker side to Maxvorstadt is its role in the Nazi years as the backdrop to parades and rallies. The NS Dokuzentrum does an excellent job of telling the story.

Getting Around

On Foot
Often the only (and quickest) way of getting around Maxvorstadt is by walking. Distances are short.

U-Bahn
The Königsplatz U-Bahn station on the U1, U2 and U8 lines delivers you to within walking distance of the sights in the Kunstareal.

Bus
Bus 100 calls at the Pinakotheken stop in the heart of the Kunstareal.

Tram
Tram 27 trundles along Barer Strasse which cuts through the Kunstareal.

★ THE BEST

WORLD-CLASS ART
Kunstareal (p64)

20TH-CENTURY HISTORY
NS Dokuzentrum (p70)

FINE DINING Jan (p76)

DRINKING WITH HISTORY
Alter Simpl (p76)

GREEN SPACE Alter Botanischer Garten (p74)

Museum Brandhorst (p65)
MATT REID/GETTY IMAGES

MAXVORSTADT

For more see

- Top Experiences ⭐ p64
- Experiences ✳ p74
- Eating ✖ p76
- Drinking 🍺 p76
- Shopping 🛍 p77

MAXVORSTADT

EXPLORE

Map labels:
- Josephsplatz
- Georgenstr
- Nordendstr
- Tschaikaistr
- Adalbertstr
- Schraudolphstr
- Barer Str
- Schwindstr
- Augustenstr
- Schellingstr
- Türkenstr
- Amalienstr
- Theresienstr
- Hessstr
- Luisenstr
- Arcisstr
- Theresienstr
- Gabelsbergerstr
- Neue Pinakothek
- Alte Pinakothek
- **Kunstareal**
- Museum Brandhorst
- Pinakothek der Moderne
- MAXVORSTADT
- enbachhaus
- Glyptothek
- **State Museum of Egyptian Art**
- önigsplatz
- Propyläen
- Königsplatz
- Antikensammlungen
- Ehrentempel
- **NS Dokuzentrum**
- **St Bonifaz Church**
- Karolinenplatz
- Ottostr
- Oskar-von-Miller-Ring
- Jägerstr
- Odeonsplatz
- Brienner Str
- Odeonsplatz
- Karlstr
- Sophienstr
- Katharina-von-Bora-Str
- Barer Str
- Max-Joseph-Str
- Maximiliansplatz
- Sonnenstr
- Pranner str
- Theatinerstr
- Residenzstr
- **Alter Botanischer Garten**
- **Justizpalast**
- Elisenstr
- Prielmayerstr
- chützenstr
- Karlsplatz
- Pacellistr
- Maxburgstr
- Promenadeplatz
- Löwengrube
- Maffeistr
- Elisenhof
- Karlsplatz
- Neuhauser Str
- ALTSTADT

63

⭐ **TOP EXPERIENCE**

Kunstareal

Munich's unrivalled Kunstareal is a compact area of Maxvorstadt packed with southern Germany's finest art museums – the Königsplatz, the Brandhorst and the Pinakotheken could keep art fans busy for days. Many travel to the Bavarian capital specifically to spend time amid these highbrow institutions.

MAP P62 **F3**

Alte Pinakothek

With its vast collection of art from the 14th to the 18th centuries, the **Alte Pinakothek** (pictured right; *pinakothek.de; adult/child €9/free*) is one of the world's top art museums and if you are going to choose just one gallery to visit in the Kunstareal, many would say this should be it. This neoclassical temple to Old European Masters was designed by Leo von Klenze as a purpose-built gallery for the Wittelsbachs' art collections, now administered by a venerable institution called the Bavarian State Painting Collections. The whole thing got a major revamp a decade or so ago, but instead of a sterile 21st-century makeover, the building's austerity and simplicity were preserved, making the whole thing an archetypal European museum experience.

Da Vinci, Cranach the Elder, Dürer, Memling, Bruegel the Elder, Rubens, Botticelli, Rafael, Titian, Velázquez, Raphael...the list of big-name European artists goes on in room after room, every work a recognised, priceless masterpiece. There are too many highlights to mention them all, though Dürer's bearded self-portrait, Rubens' monster *Great Last Judgement* and Rembrandt's *Passion Cycle* stick in the memory. At the time of

PLANNING TIP
The lawns around the Alte Pinakothek are a lovely place for a good-weather picnic lunch between galleries, though you certainly won't be alone.

Scan for everything you need to know about the Munich Kunstareal.

© BAYERISCHE STAATSGEMÄLDESAMMLUNGEN, MUNICH, ELISABETH GREIL, WWW.SCHLOESSER.BAYERN.DE

writing, some of the Alte Pinakothek was taken up by significant works from the closed Neue Pinakothek, the definite highpoint being one of Van Gogh's *Sunflowers*.

Museum Brandhorst

A bold and aptly abstract building, clad entirely in 36,000 vividly multihued ceramic tubes, the **Museum Brandhorst** *(museum-brandhorst.de; adult/child €9/free)* jostled its way into the Munich Kunstareal in a punkish blaze of colour in 2009. Its walls, floor and occasionally its ceiling provide space for some of the most challenging art in the world. Temporary shows are complimented by changing displays from the Brandhorst's own collections, which include 1200 pieces of art from the 1960s to the present day. There are many a Warhol, Hirst, Twombly and Katz.

QUICK BREAK
Both the Alte Pinakothek and the Brandhorst have good cafes. Other options are surprisingly thin on the ground for such a frequented area.

€1 SUNDAYS
Many of the Kunstareal's institutions charge only €1 admission on Sunday. This can save visitors quite a few euros but make Sunday the busiest day.

The exhibitions here change every six months to a year, so you never quite know what you are going to get. But whatever is gracing the walls, flung across the floor or draped from the ceiling, it's going to be world-class, headline-making art. Previous temporary shows have included *Alex Katz: Portraits and Landscapes; Warholmania in Munich;* and *Five Friends: John Cage, Merce Cunningham, Jasper Johns, Robert Rauschenberg, Cy Twombly.*

After your visit, there's a cool cafe in the foyer and one of the best art book shops in the northern hemisphere to peruse.

Pinakothek der Moderne

Germany's largest modern-art museum, the cavernous **Pinakothek der Moderne** (pictured

© BAYERISCHE STAATSGEMÄLDESAMMLUNGEN, MUNICH, HAYDAR KOYUPINAR, WWW.SCHLOESSER.BAYERN.DE

below; *pinakothek.de; adult/child €10/free*), brings together four museums under one roof and is therefore an engaging (and often confusing) mixed bag that has something for everyone. The exhibitions would fit into a building 10 times smaller and this is one of Munich's more exhausting museum experiences, but shows are well curated and always thought-provoking. Allow at least two hours to see just what interests you.

The **State Gallery of Modern Art** is the highlight for most, with works by Picasso, Klee, Dalí, Kandinsky, Warhol, Twombly, Flavin and Beuys. The **New Collection** is a fascinating parade of applied design with everything from VW Beetles and Eames chairs to early Apple Macs and Czech Tatra cars. The **State Graphics Collection** has 400,000 pieces of art on paper, including drawings, prints and engravings by such artists as Leonardo da Vinci and Paul Cézanne. Finally, if you make it that far, there's the **Architecture Museum**, with entire studios of drawings, blueprints, photographs and models by top practitioners such as baroque architect Balthasar Neumann and Le Corbusier.

Highlights of the Königsplatz

The original showcase for royal Wiitelsbach art established by Ludwig I, the **Königsplatz** *(antike -am-koenigsplatz.mwn.de)* boasts two grand old museum institutions. Both of the structures here, which face off over the lawns and limestone gravel, were designed by Leo von Klenze: the oh-so neoclassical **Glyptothek** is Munich's oldest museum, housing a feast of art and sculpture from ancient Greece and Rome amassed by King Ludwig I between 1806 and 1830, while the **Antikensammlungen** showcases Greek, Roman and Etruscan antiquities. The collection of Greek vases, each artistically decorated with gods and heroes, wars and weddings, is particularly outstanding. Other galleries present gold and silver jewellery

WALK OF ART
The myriad institutions of the Munich Kunstareal can be a bit overwhelming at first and it's easy to get your Pinakotheken in a twist. However, help is at hand – from the Kunstareal website *(kunstareal. de)* you can download an interactive stroll through the area with lots of info on the various things to see.

and ornaments, figurines made from terracotta and more precious bronze, and superfragile glass drinking vessels. Both museums are visited on a single **ticket** (*adult/child €6/free*). Allow around two hours to do them justice.

The Doric-columned **Propyläen** is the grand gateway to the square and on the opposite side the Nazis added the neoclassical **Ehrentempel**, containing the bodies of 16 Nazis killed in the Beer Hall Putsch. The two structures that formed the Ehrentempel were destroyed by the US Army in 1947 as part of denazification efforts and only the foundations remain fenced off at the eastern end of the square, rendered unrecognisable by foliage. There's a temporary-looking fence erected to stop the curious climbing over into the potentially dangerous site.

Lenbachhaus

At the northwest corner of the Königsplatz stands the **Lenbachhaus** (pictured right; *lenbachhaus. de; adult/child €10/free*), one of Munich's top galleries. The Lenbachhaus is named after Franz von Lenbach, a late-19th-century portrait painter who once had his studio here, a place Munich's artist community would gather. This celebrated art museum (officially the Munich Municipal Art Gallery) specialises in vibrant canvases by Wassily Kandinsky, Franz Marc, Paul Klee and other members of ground-breaking modernist group Der Blaue Reiter (The Blue Rider), founded in Munich in 1911. The gallery also puts on shows of contemporary and modern art and its collections include works by Gerhard Richter, Sigmar Polke, Anselm Kiefer, Andy Warhol, Dan Flavin, Richard Serra and Jenny Holzer.

Tickets are also valid for special exhibits at the nearby Kunstbau, a 120m-long tunnel above the Königsplatz U-Bahn station accessible directly from

FURTHER EXPLORATION

Here we have listed the biggest attractions in the Kunstareal, but the show goes on in 26 other galleries, museums and venerable institutions. If you visited one a day, you'd need over a month to see everything from 5000-year-old Egyptian art to contemporary installations created while you were on the plane to Germany. The Kunstareal website *(kunstareal.de)* has the full list.

MARIANGELA CRUZ/SHUTTERSTOCK

it. This was added a decade ago to a design by British architect Norman Foster, but some regard it as one vanity gallery too far in the Kunstareal.

Neue Pinakothek – Closed
It wouldn't be possible to talk about the Munich Kunstareal without mentioning the **Neue Pinakothek**. Housing the city's collection of van Goghs, Turners and Monets, it took its turn to close for renovation in 2019 (after the long closure of the Alte Pinakothek) and had been scheduled to reopen in 2025 at the latest. However, in 2022 the authorities dropped a bombshell when they put that date back a full four years to 2029. This means that by the time it reopens, the museum will have been closed for an entire decade. Many claim this is an unacceptable length of time for such a major visitor attraction to be shut.

OPEN & CLOSED
Many institutions in the Kunstareal are closed on Monday but almost all have one night a week when they open late.

★ TOP EXPERIENCE

NS Dokuzentrum

Where did the Nazis come from, how did Hitler seize power and why Munich? Free to enter, the excellent NS Dokuzentrum attempts to answer these questions and many more in an expertly curated exhibition. It also examines why Germany has found this period so difficult to process.

MAP P62 **F4**

Hitler & Munich

In May 1913 an anonymous failed Austrian artist arrived to take up residence in Munich. Returning after Germany's defeat in WWI, Adolf Hitler entered politics, joining the German Workers' Party. As a charismatic rabble rouser, Hitler soon rose to the top of the party, giving his famously vitriolic beer hall speeches. In 1923 the failed Beer Hall Putsch landed Hitler in Landsberg prison, where he penned *Mein Kampf* during his year of incarceration. German economic woes provided fertile ground for Hitler's anti-Jewish rhetoric, and millions began to follow him. In 1933 the first concentration camp opened in Dachau. In 1934 Hitler became Germany's head of state. The Führer had big plans to rebuild Munich, but managed only the Haus der Kunst and a few buildings around the Königsplatz.

Documenting the Role in the Rise of Hitler

It is near the Königsplatz that the **NS Dokuzentrum** *(National Socialism Documentation Centre; ns-dokuzentrum-muenchen.de; free)* strives to educate locals and visitors alike about the Nazi period and Munich's oft misunderstood role in it. The excellent permanent exhibition entitled Munich and National Socialism attempts to find answers to questions about why Hitler came to power, what

PLANNING TIP
Due to the subject matter, the NS Dokuzentrum does not recommend children under 14 visit. This holds true for most WWII-related sites.

Scan for full opening hours and other details.

© NS-DOKUMENTATIONSZENTRUM MÜNCHEN, FOTO: CONNOLLY WEBER

led to WWII and why democracy failed. Period documents, artefacts, films and multimedia stations help visitors form their own understanding. The NSDAP (National Socialist German Workers' Party) was established in Munich after all, and the city was affected by the early years of Hitler's rise to power like no other in Germany. At first, much of the Nazi brand took from southern German folk culture, associations which have been hard to throw off.

Temporary Shows

In addition to the permanent exhibition there are often superb temporary shows on a Nazi, WWII or general human rights and injustice theme. Shows in the past have focused on the Warsaw Ghetto, Russia's war in Ukraine and forced labour under the Nazis.

QUICK BREAK
The museum cafe at the Alte Pinakothek (p64) or the stylish cafe within the Brandhorst (p65) are the best places for a coffee or light meal near the NS Dokuzentrum.

Walk Maxvorstadt

Maxvorstadt is all about big-name art and Nazi buildings, right? Well, even this small Munich neighbourhood has a B side, the grid of streets west of the Königsplatz and the Pinakotheken serve up some wonderfully distinctive but wholly unvisited sights. Uncover a part of Munich few except the locals know.

START	END	LENGTH
Alter Botanischer Garten	Nordbard	4km, two hours

1 Botanical Garden

The **Alter Botanischer Garten** (p74) is a pleasant, rather bushy park centred around a large Neptune-themed fountain – a verdant oasis in a traffic-heavy part of town. There are acres of bench space here for picnickers or you could head to the Park Cafe (p76), a beer garden frequented by locals.

2 Neo-Renaissance Church

Established by King Ludwig I in 1835, the red-brick and stone **St Bonifaz Church** (p75) is fronted by eight classical columns. That's unusual enough in Munich, but the interior is an even bigger surprise: the pews form a circle around the altar, there is abstract art on the walls and the organ looks like it's made from bits of BMW engine.

3 A Wanderable Thoroughfare

Arrow-straight **Augustenstrasse** is lined with cafes, bakeries, secondhand shops, falafel joints and Turkish barbers. Standout places include Cafe Jasmin (p77), where the retro interior takes you back to the days of the *Wirtschaftswunder* (West Germany's postwar economic recovery). The Munich Readery (p77), Germany's best English secondhand bookshop, is also at the northern end.

4 Munich's 'Other' University

Turning out graduates that contribute to the country's engineering prowess, **Munich Technical University** is one of Germany's best. Come here for the modern rooftop **Café im Vorhoelzer Forum**, which has some of the best views of any Munich eatery (if it happens to be open to non-students/staff).

5 Alter Nordfriedhof

You might think this overgrown graveyard was the last place you'd want to hang out. However, the joggers, mums with prams, and running kids give the game away. After just 71 years, the Nazis decommissioned this 19th-century cemetery, and following WWII it became a park but the gravestones stayed... There are 800 tombs here, some belonging to members of the German resistance including one Weisse Rose member.

6 Josephsplatz

Dominating Josephsplatz, the neo-baroque **St Joseph Church** looks older than it is, having only been built in 1898. Inside, it's a mammoth barrel of whitewashed stucco. Outside, there is an interesting children's **playground**, and there's a small food market most days.

7 Swimming Pool

The **Nordbad** is a Munich swimming pool with an old exterior but fully modernised inside. It's one of the least frequented pools and is open from very early morning till late at night. Tram 27 runs back to the city centre from here.

EXPERIENCES

Find your Mummie at the State Museum of Egyptian Art
EGYPTIAN HISTORY

MAP: ❶ P62 **F4**

If you fancy a change of tack from all the tortured artistic souls of 19th- and 20th-century art, the **State Museum of Egyptian Art** *(smaek.de; adult/child €7/free)* is located on the Königsplatz. Completely rebuilt a decade ago, this well-curated, atmospherically illuminated concrete slab of a museum traces 5000 years of Egyptian and Sudanese history in one of the finest collections in Europe. Descending into the bowels of the building is like delving into an Egyptian tomb beneath a pyramid, one packed with mummies, sarcophagi, ancient jewellery, sculpture and everyday items. It's a great place to bring the kids (who get in free) if they happen to be going through an Ancient Egypt phase.

Relax at Alter Botanischer Garten
CITY-CENTRE GREENERY

MAP: ❷ P62 **E5**

Often overlooked by visitors to Munich, the **Alter Botanischer Garten** (Old Botanical Garden) is a pleasant place to soothe soles and souls after an Altstadt shopping spree or to see out a long wait for a train away from the Hauptbahnhof. Created under King Maximilian in 1814, most of the tender specimens were moved in the early 20th century to the New Botanical Garden behind Schloss Nymphenburg, leaving this verdant, city-centre breathing space.

The **Neptunbrunnen** (Neptune Fountain), on the south side, dates from the Nazi period when the garden was turned into a public park. The flower arrangements here are often spectacular, especially in the spring months. The neoclassical entrance gate is called the **Kleine Propyläen** and is a leftover from the original gardens. The Old

---

 BUS 100 – MUSEENLINIE

By far the most useful bus route in Munich's city centre is the 100, aka Museenlinie, that makes 18 stops between the Ostbahnhof and the Hauptbahnhof, and links more than 20 museums and other interesting localities en route. The Königsplatz, Lenbachhaus, the Kunstareal, Haus der Kunst, the Englischer Garten, Eisbachwelle, Villa Stuck and the Bavarian National Museum are all connected by this ordinary Stadtbus (city bus). Leaving every 10 minutes in both directions (every 20 minutes on weekends), the 100 also serves as a kind of budget hop-on, hop-off route, especially if you already have a day pass.

Botanical Garden is also home to one of Munich's lower-profile beer gardens, Park Cafe (p76).

On the northern side of the park stands the **Kunstpavillon** *(kunst pavillion.org)* where small, free art exhibitions take place.

Discover the tomb of King Ludwig I
CHURCH

MAP: ③ P62 **E5**

In addition to its unusual circular pew layout and ultra-modern inventory, Maxvorstadt's **St Bonifaz Church** is also the resting place of a few Wittelsbachs, including one Ludwig I. The king who arguably left the greatest mark of any Wittelsbach on Munich – he had a vision of turning the capital into 'Athens on the Isar' – died in Nice in 1868, 20 years after abdicating and was buried here with his wife Therese of Saxe-Hildburghausen (the queen whose marriage to Ludwig I kicked off the Oktoberfest). The large marble sarcophagus is on the right as you enter. Behind the church is a Benedictine monastery built between 1835 and 1850 under King Ludwig I. The king chose this site rather than the traditional final resting place of the Wittelsbachs in the Theatinerkirche as he wished to rest among the Benedictines who he had returned to the capital.

Visit a Notorious Courtroom
HISTORICAL SITE

MAP: ④ P62 **E6**

The 1890s **Justizpalast** witnessed the Weisse Rose trial of Hans Scholl, Sophie Scholl and Christoph Probst on 22 February 1943. Condemned to death by judge Roland Freisler, the verdict was read at 1pm and four hours later they were dead. There's a permanent exhibit about the sham trial in the very courtroom (room 253) where it took place.

Neptunbrunnen

LISTINGS

Best Places for...

€ Budget €€ Midrange €€€ Top End

See p62 for map of locations

Eating

Going Local

Wirtshaus Obacht €€
5 E2

This modern, evenings-only tavern specialises in all things southern German, so expect lots of *Spätzle*, roast meat and dumplings, all traditional, but often done with a modern twist. Vegetarians and vegans are well catered for. *5pm-midnight*

Steinheil 16 €€
6 E3

Studenty feeding and watering spot just off Augustenstrasse serving *Currywurst,* schnitzel, big salads and lots of meat- and dairy-free food on retro-styled furniture. The walls are adorned by local artists. *11am-1am*

Vegetarian & Vegan

Sankt Annas €€
 E3

Alpine vegan is not a restaurant type you hear very often but this crisply designed, modern place offers meat- and dairy-free versions of South Tyrolean favourites as well as filling options such as porridge and burgers. *11am-10pm Tue-Sun*

Cafe Ignaz €€
 F1

Surprisingly good neighbourhood spot for some vegetarian and vegan food, with quirky artwork on the walls, a tightly packed interior and a few benches outside. *11.30am-10pm Wed-Fri, 10am-9pm Sat & Sun*

Non-Bavarian Eats

Il Mulino €€
 F1

This much-loved neighbourhood classic has been feeding Italophiles and immigrants from the beautiful country for over three decades. All the expected pastas and pizzas are present and correct. *11.30am-midnight*

Jan €€€
 E5

With his seven-course tasting menu, chef Jan Hartwig has earned an incredible three Michelin stars through a real labour of love. Bagging a table in the spartan dining room will be your labour of love, too. *evenings Tue-Thu, lunch & evenings Fri*

Drinking

Pubs, Beer Halls & Beer Gardens

Alter Simpl
11 H2

Thomas Mann and Hermann Hesse used to knock 'em back at this well-scuffed and wood-panelled thirst parlour. A bookish ambience still pervades, making this an apt spot at which to curl up with a weighty tome. *11.30am-midnight*

Park Cafe
 E5

A bit of a hidden gem, this typical Munich beer garden in the Alter Botanischer Garten serves Hofbräu lager and lots of filling food. *11am-11pm*

Augustiner Keller
 C5

This 5000-seat beer garden west of the Hauptbahnhof buzzes with fairy-lit, thirst-quenching activity from the first sign that spring may have *gesprungen*. *10am-midnight*

Löwenbräukeller
14 D4

Beer hall and garden at the Löwenbräu Brewery, one Munich's traditional lager producers. *11am-midnight*

Die Kneipe 80
15 G3

Next to the Alte Pinakothek, this small pub is strategically located for those who have worked up a thirst (and a hunger) in the nearby galleries. *2pm-late*

Coffee & Cocktails
Cafe Jasmin
 E3

Take a trip back to the confident heyday of the Federal Republic at this *echt*-retro stalwart of the Maxvorstadt espresso scene that's been serving coffee, cocktails and light meals since 1950. Said to be Mick Jagger's favourite cafe when he's in town. *10am-1am*

Shopping

English Books
Munich Readery
 E2

With Germany's biggest collection of second-hand English-language titles, the Readery is the place to go in Bavaria for holiday reading matter. In fact we think this might be the only such second-hand bookshop between Paris and Prague. *11am-8pm Mon-Fri, to 6pm Sat*

Trachten & Dirndl
Holareidulijö
 F2

One of the best second-hand Lederhosen and Dirndl resellers in Munich and been around for some years. Call ahead for an appointment as the shop has no opening hours.

Daller Tracht
19 D3

Small shop selling traditional frilly frocks and Lederhosen that every Bavarian keeps in their wardrobe for special occasions, and foreigners buy to attend Oktoberfest. *10am-6pm Mon-Sat*

★ WORTH A TRIP

KZ-Gedenkstätte Dachau

A short S-Bahn ride from central Munich, the small town of Dachau is infamous as the site of the Nazis' first concentration camp, established in 1933 and a blueprint for the many that followed. Needless to say, a visit is a thought-provoking experience.

Horrific First

Officially called the KZ-Gedenkstätte Dachau, this was the Nazis' first concentration camp, created in 1933 to incarcerate pretty much anyone the Nazis disliked. Later inmates from all over Europe were imprisoned here and in the many subcamps that were set up across Bavaria. All in all, Dachau 'processed' over 200,000 inmates, killing at least 41,500. Dachau KZ was used for another two decades as 'temporary' accommodation for Sudeten Germans at the end of WWII. It only became a memorial site in the mid-1960s.

Touring the Dachau Camp

Expect to spend two to three hours here to fully absorb the exhibits. Note this is not a place to bring children or even teenagers.

Start at the visitors centre, where you can pick up an audioguide or join a 2½-hour English-language tour at 11am and 1pm.

You pass into the compound itself through the Jourhaus (entrance building) – set in wrought iron, the infamous, chilling slogan *'Arbeit Macht Frei'* (Work Sets You Free) hits you at the gate.

The museum is at the southern end of the camp. Here, a 38-minute film (in English at 10.15am, 11.45am and 2pm) tells the story of the camp through eyewitness accounts. Either side of the

GETTING THERE
To reach the camp, take the S-Bahn (S2) to Dachau Bahnhof then bus 726 from outside the station to the KZ-Gedenkstätte stop. An M1 ticket is needed and the journey takes around 40 minutes.

Scan for comprehensive information relating to the Dachau camp memorial.

RAIVO SARELAINENS/GETTY IMAGES

small cinema extends an exhibition on the camp's harrowing story. Some of the displays are extremely disturbing but form the core of all visits.

Outside, in the former roll-call square, is the International Memorial (1968), inscribed in English, French, Yiddish, German and Russian, which reads 'Never Again'. Behind the exhibit building, the bunker was he notorious camp prison where inmates were tortured. Executions took place in the prison yard.

Inmates were housed in large barracks that lined the main road north of the roll-call square. These are all now demolished except two which contain mock-ups of the dorms and washrooms. Outside the camp perimeter fence to the northwest stands the crematorium and gas chamber, the latter disguised as a shower room but never used. Several religious sites have been built nearby.

QUICK BREAK
The only place to eat here is the self-service cafeteria within the visitors centre, which serves surprisingly reasonably priced meals and drinks.

See p94 for eating, drinking and shopping listings

Explore
Schwabing & the Englischer Garten

Once the gritty, bohemian haunt of world-class artists and artisans, Schwabing long since completed its journey to neatly renovated gentrification. Very few hints that this grid of streets north of the Altstadt was ever anything other than a middle-class hip hangout of vintage-clothes shops and cool cafes remain. Some streets do have a decidedly student vibe, though few students can actually afford to live near Munich's university, which is also here.

More a place for aimless wandering, people-watching and window shopping, there are some worthwhile sights here. The rambling Bayerisches Nationalmuseum and the Haus der Kunst are indoor highlights, and running down Schwabing's eastern flank is Munich's green lung, the Englischer Garten.

Getting Around

 On Foot
The best way to get around Schwabing's grid of streets and the paths of the Englischer Garten is to walk. Other than biking it, in the Englischer Garten you actually have no other choice.

 U-Bahn
The U3 and the U6 stop at Universität, Giselastrasse and Münchner Freiheit in the east of the neighbourhood on the edge of the Englischer Garten.

 Bus
Bus 100 cuts through the neighbourhood on its way between the Ostbahnhof and the Hauptbahnhof.

Englischer Garten (p84)
ALBERTO MASNOVO/SHUTTERSTOCK

THE BEST

CITY GREENERY Englischer Garten (p84)

STUDENT LIFE Ludwig-Maximilians-Universität (p88)

WEIGHTY COLLECTIONS Bayerisches Nationalmuseum (p89)

TOP BEER GARDEN Chinesischer Turm (p95)

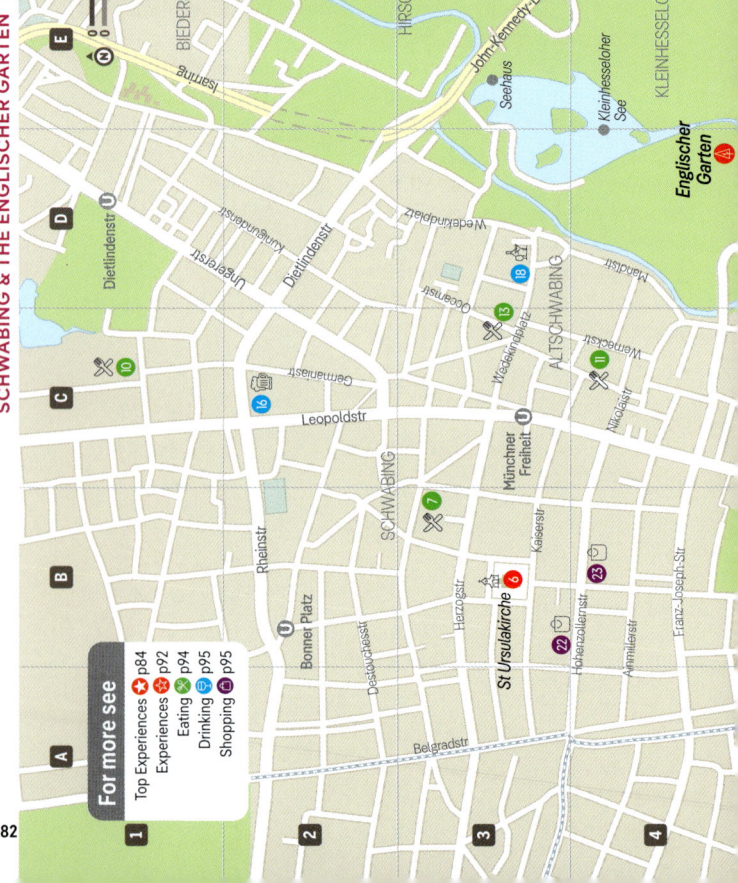

SCHWABING & THE ENGLISCHER GARTEN

EXPLORE

★ TOP EXPERIENCE

Englischer Garten

The sprawling English Garden is among Europe's biggest city parks – it even rivals London's Hyde Park and New York's Central Park for size – and is a popular playground for locals and visitors alike. It's a superb place to laze around but has several attractions, too.

MAP P82 **D4**

PLANNING TIP
If you are short on time, some Munich tour agencies run cycling tours of the Englischer Garten. **Mike's Bike Tours** (mikesbiketours.com) are the most popular.

Scan for further information on the Englischer Garten.

A Little History
Stretching north from Prinzregentenstrasse for about 5km, Munich's city park was commissioned by Elector Karl Theodor in 1789 and designed by Benjamin Thompson, an American-born British scientist working as an adviser to the Bavarian government. Initially a park designed for use by the army, it was later opened up for the public. A prime piece of real estate worth billions, to this day nothing can be built here.

Monopteros
Rising above the main lawns of the Englischer Garten is the **Monopteros** (1838), a faux Greek temple. There are no prizes for guessing which monarch had a Greek temple built in a public park – yes, that's right, Ludwig I commissioned the structure in honour of Elector Karl Theodor, though he never saw it finished. It was designed by Ludwig I's favourite architect Leo von Klenze. Apart from the architecture there are two reasons to come here. First is that, although not a particularly high location, the Monopteros has a great skyline panorama of the city centre. The other reason is to hang out here with Münchners, beer in hand as the sun goes down.

WIRESTOCK CREATORS/SHUTTERSTOCK

Chinese Tower Beer Garden

A short walk north of the Monopteros brings you to the **Chinesischer Turm** (Chinese Tower; pictured above), a contender for Munich's oddest folly. It was built in the late 18th century at the same time as the park was laid out and originally served as a viewing tower. The timber tower burnt down during WWII, but was rebuilt as you see it today in 1952.

If having a Chinese Tower here was strange enough, even more unusual is that this is the unlikely setting for what many regard as Munich's best beer garden (see p95). Typical slatted tables and chairs are set out around the base of the tower and fill every evening with drinkers. On a humid summer's evening it's one of the best places to find yourself, tankard in hand.

QUICK BREAK
The incredibly popular **Fräulein Grüneis kiosk** (p94) is the best place to go for a quick coffee, beer, cake or sandwich.

THE WALL
A section of the Berlin Wall lurks hidden between the Haus der Kunst (p92) and the US Consulate. A gift from Berlin, it was placed there in 1996.

Urban Surfing

At the far southern end of the park, the main attraction is the **Eisbachwelle**, an artificially created wave in the Eisbach where wetsuit-clad daredevils 'hang 10', quite an unusual sight in a European city centre. The wave reopened in June 2025 after an accident (see opposite).

Japanese Teahouse

Once you've seen the Chinese Tower, another hint of Asia awaits further south at the **Japanisches Teehaus** *(urasenke-muenchen.de)*, built for the 1972 Olympics next to an idyllic duck pond. The best time to come is for an authentic tea ceremony celebrated by a Japanese tea master, though it's only open two days a month. Check the website for which days those are going to be.

DAGMAR BREU/SHUTTERSTOCK

Heading North

The further north you go, the wilder the Englischer Garten becomes, though there are two spots where nature has been tamed for human enjoyment. The **Kleinhesseloher See** (pictured left) is a lovely lake where you can boat around three little islands, then reward your efforts with a beer at the slightly upmarket **Seehaus**. Some day soon a tunnel will take the motorway just north of the lake under the greenery, reuniting the two halves of the park. For now a footbridge is needed to reach the **Hirschau** (p95) beer garden, one of Munich's best.

Kicking Back

The English Garden may have its attractions, but the main activities here play out on the huge lawns and paths around them, especially in the central section of the park. The Englischer Garten has an incredible 78km of paths and most of them are flat. That makes for the ideal place to train for that running event or just take a leisurely city-centre jog. Cycling is also popular, though stay out of the way of Munich's velocommuters who can speed their way through the park in quite a dangerous manner. The lawns below the Monopteros (the so-called Monowiese) are a hive of activity when the sun shines – students laze revising on the grass, kids run circles through the picnicking throngs and van lifers chase Frisbees into the bushes. At dusk this part of the park can resemble an impromptu party with many a bottled Tegernseer and Paulaner opened on the lawns.

EISBACH TRAGEDY

At the southern tip of the Englischer Garten, surfers have always braved the freezing waters of the single-wave Eisbach that surges from under a bridge. However, in April 2025, a 33-year-old surfer died after snagging her board leash on an unidentified object. It was originally thought this would be curtains for the wave, but in June the same year the Eisbachwelle reopened albeit with much stricter rules: surfers cannot surf alone, boards must have a quick-release or self-releasing leash. Hours are limited to 5.30am to 10pm and only fit, competent surfers can take to the wave.

★ TOP EXPERIENCE

Ludwig-Maximilians-Universität

Bavaria's oldest university, the Ludwig-Maximilians-Universität started life in Ingolstadt in 1472, later moving to Landshut in 1800 before being shifted to Munich in 1826 by King Ludwig I. It has produced over a dozen Nobel Prize winners, including Wilhelm Röntgen in 1901 (Physics) and Theodor Hänsch in 2005 (Physics).

MAP P82 **B6**

DenkStätte Weisse Rose

The main building, designed by Ludwig I's second favourite architect Friedrich von Gärtner, has cathedral-like dimensions and is accented with sculpture and other artworks. However, the main story here is that of the **Weisse Rose** (p93), the Nazi resistance group founded by Hans and Sophie Scholl who were students here at the time. Outside the entrance there appear to be various papers and pamphlets strewn across the cobbles. These are concrete facsimiles of the Scholls' leaflets, newspaper reports and alike from the time, set into the pavement.

Enter the building and cross the atrium to a flight of stairs that leads down to a single room dedicated to a solemn but modernly conceived memorial to Die Weisse Rose. The free exhibition tells the story of their peaceful resistance and maps their fate at the hands of the Gestapo. Fittingly, the address of the uni is Geschwister-Scholl-Platz – the circular Scholl Siblings Square.

PLANNING TIP
The DenkStätte Weisse Rose keeps relatively short hours. It is open 10.30am to 4.30pm Monday to Friday and 11.30am to 4pm Saturday, so time visits accordingly.

Studenty Bites

The best place in these parts to join the undergraduates of Munich for a cuppa and a sarnie is the uni cafe called **Cadu (Cafe an der Uni)**, which spills out onto Ludwigstrasse. It's a great place to while away a rainy afternoon with a book or your laptop; see p94.

Scan for further information on Munich's university.

 **TOP EXPERIENCE**

Bayerisches Nationalmuseum

This classic 19th-century museum is a palatial neoclassical edifice overflowing with exotic treasures and works of art, a repository for a nation's history, and a grand, purpose-built display case for royal trinkets, church baubles and state-owned rarities.

MAP P82 **D8**

One of Germany's Biggest Museums

The collection at the **Bavarian National Museum** (*bayerisches-nationalmuseum.de; adult/child €7/ free*) fills 40 rooms over three floors. There's a lot to get through, so be prepared for at least two hours' legwork. Exhibitions cover everything from antiquity to 20th-century design.

Most visitors start on the 1st floor, where hall after hall is packed with baroque, mannerist and Renaissance sculpture, ecclesiastical treasures (check out all those wobbly dancing Gothic 'S' figures), Renaissance clothing and one-off pieces such as the 1000-year-old St Kunigunde's chest, fashioned in mammoth ivory and gold.

Climb to the 2nd floor to move up in history to the rococo, Jugendstil and modern periods, represented by priceless collections of Nymphenburg and Meissen porcelain, Tiffany glass, Augsburg silver and precious items used by the Bavarian royal family. Also up here is a huge circular model of Munich in the first half of the 19th century, shortly after it was transformed into a capital fit for a kingdom.

Temporary Exhibitions & Shop

Top-notch temporary exhibitions are also held, very often on themes relating to the history of Bavaria and/or Munich. The ticket to these costs extra. The excellent museum shop is one of the best in Bavaria.

PLANNING TIP
The Bavarian National Museum is one of the Munich cultural institutions that charges a symbolic €1 on Sundays. However, this does not apply to the temporary shows.

Scan for full opening hours and ticket prices.

Walk Schwabing

Centred around the university and the Academy of Fine Arts, this erstwhile bolthole for 19th- and early-20th-century artists and writers still has a bohemian feel, despite postwar gentrification. Join the students for a bite to eat, peruse vintage-clothes shops and admire the Art Nouveau architecture.

START	END	LENGTH
Ludwig-Maximilians-Universität	Wedekind-Platz	3km, 1¾ hours

1 Munich Uni

From morning till dusk the area around **Ludwig-Maximilians-Universität** (p88) bustles with students, many of whom tie up their rattling two-wheelers along Ludwigstrasse. The top attraction for visitors within the uni building is the DenkStätte Weisse Rose.

2 Cafes & Books

Running next to the uni, **Schellingstrasse** funnels students to various watering and feeding spots. In addition to many cafes, it's also the location of **Words' Worth Books** (p95), the city's best English bookstore, and the uni bookshop.

3 Lunch Spot

Running north–south, **Amalienstrasse** bustles with cafes, delis and restaurants that serve a multitude of cuisines lining its arrow-straight length. It's one of the best places to head for lunch, though gets very busy with hungry students.

4 Shops & Famed Drinking Hole

Make your way over to **Türkenstrasse**, home to interesting shops, including those stocking antiques and vintage clothes, and even an Oxfam shop at No 81. But the highlight here is **Alter Simpl** (p76), one of Munich's most famous pubs where Thomas Mann, Hermann Hesse and other Schwabing writers, poets and artists once drank.

5 Neighbourhood Park

Take a break at **Leopoldpark**, good for children with its large playground. Normally packed with students from the nearby Academy of Fine Arts lazing on the grass or writing a last-minute essay, it's a relaxing place to soak up the atmosphere.

6 Literary History

Schwabing becomes more gentrified the further north you stroll, but it wasn't that way when Wassily Kandinsky and Rainer Maria Rilke lived at Nos 36 and 34 respectively on **Ainmillerstrasse**. Seek out their brass plaques and admire the perfectly renovated Art Nouveau facades.

7 Neo-Renaissance Church

Often called the 'Cathedral of Schwabing', **St Ursula's Church** (p93) on Kaiserplatz is an impressive wedge of neo-Renaissance dating from 1897. The church is 100% original having suffered virtually no bomb damage in WWII.

8 Nightlife Hotspot

Beyond the Münchner Freiheit transport hub, the area around **Wedekind-Platz** is a nightlife hotspot, with bars, cafes and quirky German-language comedy theatres. On Wedekind-Platz, look out for the crooked lamp post, the Schwabinger Laterne, once made famous by local chanson singer, Schwabinger Gisela.

EXPERIENCES

Peek into the Nazis' Haus der Kunst
ART GALLERY

MAP: ① P82 **C8**

On the edge of the Englischer Garten, the infamous **Haus der Kunst** *(hausderkunst.de; admission varies according to exhibition)* sits behind an austere fascist-era edifice that was built in 1937 (Hitler himself laid the foundation stone) to showcase Nazi art. Designed by Hitler's favourite architect Paul Ludwig Troost, this is one of the few surviving examples of Nazi neoclassicism in the Bavarian capital. The monumental limestone facade features Roman columns and rigid symmetry so typical of fascist-era architecture.

These days the Haus der Kunst presents works by the type of artists whom the Nazis rejected and deemed degenerate. The museum has no collections of its own, acting solely as a venue for temporary shows of contemporary art and design. At night, the Goldene Bar (p95) here is one Munich's most impressive cocktail spots.

Appreciate Von Gärtner's Neoclassical Opus
CHURCH

MAP: ② P82 **B6**

On the southeastern side of Geschwister-Scholl-Platz rise the sombre neoclassical twin-towers of the **Ludwigskirche** *(st-ludwig-muenchen.de),* built by Friedrich von Gärtner between 1829 and 1844. One of Munich's more unusual churches, it is a highly decorative, almost Byzantine, affair with one major showpiece: the huge *Last Judgment* fresco by the Nazarene painter Peter Cornelius in the choir which completely dwarves the main altar. It's one of the largest in the world and an immodest – and thoroughly unsuccessful – attempt to outdo Michelangelo's version. The Ludwigskirche was bombed during WWII sustaining heavy damage.

Check the website for times when mass is held, an atmospheric experience.

Visit Bavaria's Top Art School
SIGNIFICANT BUILDING

MAP: ③ P82 **B5**

The **Akademie der Bildenden Künste** (Academy of Fine Arts) is housed in a three-storey neo-Renaissance palace. You can wander in to take a look around but there are no tours. Famous former students include Max Slevogt, Franz von Lenbach and Wilhelm Leibl, and early-20th-century students Lovis Corinth, Paul Klee, Wassily Kandinsky, Franz Marc and others who would go on to become modern-art pioneers.

Interestingly, the academy holds exhibitions within the Universität U-Bahn station (at the Akademiestrasse exit). This includes an end-of-semester show by students and temporary displays on various themes. This is usually only open in the afternoons.

Marvel at a von Klenze Masterpiece   SIGNIFICANT BUILDING

MAP: 4 P82 B8

Odeonsplatz marks the beginning of the Maxvorstadt, a 19th-century quarter built to link central Munich with Schwabing to the north. Leo von Klenze masterminded its overall design and several of the buildings, including the **Leuchtenberg-Palais**, a stately town palace modelled after a Roman palazzo and now home of the Bavarian Finance Ministry.

See Munich's Very Own Arc de Triomphe   LANDMARK

MAP: 5 P82 B5

Around 200m north of Geschwister-Scholl-Platz, the huge **Siegestor** was modelled on the Arch of Constantine in Rome and looks like a miniature version of the Arc de Triomphe in Paris. Built to honour the Bavarian army for sending Napoleon packing, it's crowned by a triumphant Bavaria piloting a lion-drawn chariot. Severely damaged in WWII, the arch was turned into a peace memorial. The inscription on the upper section reads: *Dem Sieg geweiht, vom Kriege zerstört, zum Frieden mahnend* (Dedicated to victory, destroyed by war, calling for peace), a very apt message still today.

Admire the Architecture of the St Ursulakirche   CHURCH

MAP: 6 P82 B3

Sometimes dubbed the 'Schwabing Cathedral', **St Ursulakirche**, anchoring the heart of the neighbourhood, is a recent addition to the Munich architectural treasure trove, having only appeared here in 1897. Built largely in the neo-Renaissance style, it sports a 64m-tall tower with Venetian spire and many other architectural features you won't find anywhere else in the Bavarian capital, blending Historicism with Art Nouveau and Modernism.

 THE WEISSE ROSE MOVEMENT

One of the few groups to rebel against the Nazis was the Weisse Rose (White Rose), led by Munich University student siblings Hans and Sophie Scholl. The nonviolent movement began operating in 1942, its members stealing out at night to smear 'Freedom!' and 'Down with Hitler!' on the city's walls. Soon they were distributing anti-Nazi leaflets. In February 1943, Hans and Sophie were caught distributing leaflets at the university. Together with best friend, Christoph Probst, the Scholls were arrested, found guilty of treason and beheaded. Their extraordinary courage inspired the award-winning film *Sophie Scholl – Die Letzten Tage* (Sophie Scholl – The Final Days; 2005).

LISTINGS

Best Places for...

€ Budget €€ Midrange €€€ Top End

See p82 for map of locations

Eating

Lunch & Brunch

Emmi's Kitchen €
7 B3
One of three Emmi's vegan superfood restaurants where all the dishes are inspired by the owner's travels. Expect lots of tofu, avocado, plant-based burgers and cake on your plate. *9am-5pm*

Türkenhof €
8 B6
This studenty resto-pub is a great stop-off for a no-fuss lunch of typical Bavarian meat and carbohydrate combos. Hip decor and friendly, non-flustered staff. *11am-midnight*

Cafe Zeitgeist €
9 B6
Great bistro-cafe serving light lunches to tourists and students. Shady courtyard with people-watching possibilities. *9am-midnight*

Gourmet Finds

Tantris €€€
10 C1
This double-Michelin-starred, psychedelic 1970s retro-resto is one of Germany's best-known restaurants. Head chef Benjamin Chmura is known for creating culinary perfection with seasonal ingredients. Book weeks ahead. *noon-4pm & 6.30-midnight Wed-Sat*

Werneckhof €€€
11 C4
Upmarket international restaurant with a Michelin twinkler serving top-quality, somewhat exotic gourmet-portioned fish and meat dishes as full-course menus. A real treat but booking ahead is essential. *noon-4pm & 6.30pm-midnight Wed-Sat*

Cheap Eats

Fräulein Grüneis €
12 D8
Madly popular kiosk near the Eisbachwelle serving coffees, homemade-style cakes, sandwiches and usually two light mains (cod and pasta when we visited). Just a couple of tables but a very friendly welcome. *8am-dusk Mon-Fri, 10am-dusk Sat & Sun*

Ruff's Burger €
13 C3
When all you want is a filling burger between sights or shops, the 100% Bavarian beef and veggie versions do the trick every time. *noon-10pm*

Cadu (Cafe an der Uni) €
14 B6
Anytime is a good time to be at studenty, charismatic Cadu. Enjoy breakfast (served until a hangover-friendly 10pm!), a cuppa Java or a Helles in the lovely garden hidden by a wall from busy Ludwigstrasse. *11am-1am Mon-Thu, to 2am Fri, 10.30am-2am Sat & Sun*

Schall & Rauch €
15 B6
The few battered cafe chairs and vintage bar-stools get bagged quickly at this small, friendly, open-fronted bar-resto, meaning drinkers often spill out onto Schelling-

strasse even during the day. The menu is an international smorgasbord and the drinks card long and refreshing. *11am-1am*

Drinking

Cocktails & Bars

Pils Doktor
 C2

An all-night cult pub in the north of Schwabing where the focus is firmly on alcoholic beverages and boozy conversation till the early hours. *6pm-late*

Goldene Bar
 C8

At the Haus Der Kunst, this spectacular, low-lit, explorer-themed bar is centred around a huge modernist chandelier. There's a summer terrace. *noon-8pm Mon, to midnight Wed & Thu, to 2am Fri & Sat, 1-8pm Sun*

Cocktailhouse
 D3

This Schwabing classic has been mixing drinks for more than 30 years and is a great spot to start a night out or for longer lingering. *7pm-late*

Beer Halls & Gardens

Chinesischer Turm
 D5

For many Munich's best beer garden, with tables and fairy lights gathered around the Chinese Tower folly in the English Garden. Large-scale food service and Hofbräu lager. *11am-10pm*

Hirschau
 F3

Mammoth beer garden in the northern half of the Englischer Garten boasting 1700 seats and live music almost every day in the summer months. When the picnic is over, dispatch the kids to the large playground while you indulge in some tankard caressing. *noon-10pm*

Shopping

English Books

Words' Worth Books
 B6

You'll find heaps of English-language books, from secondhand novels to the latest bestsellers, at this excellent and long-established bookstore. *10am-7pm Mon-Fri, to 4pm Sat*

Antiques

Kunst Oase
 B3

A treasure trove of lamps, plant stands, trinkets, keepsakes and picture frames with thousands of items on sale, all antiques and all originals. *9am-7.30pm Mon-Sat*

Clothing

Dear Goods
B4

The women's branch of this vegan clothing store is a light-filled space sprinkled with all kinds of casual, high-quality eco-fashion. *10am-8pm Mon-Fri, to 6.30pm Sat*

★ WORTH A TRIP

Schleissheim Palaces

Once you've exhausted all possibilities in central Munich, the northern suburb of Schleissheim is well worth the short S-Bahn ride for its three elegant palaces and a high-flying aviation museum. Allow at least half a day to see everything here.

GETTING THERE
Reach the palaces and museum by taking the S1 S-Bahn to Oberschleissheim (23 minutes). From the station it is a 15-minute walk south to the palaces. Flugwerft is another 10 minutes south.

Scan for full opening hours and other information regarding the palaces.

Neues Schloss Schleissheim

Top dog among Schleissheim's palatial offerings is the **Neues Schloss Schleissheim** (pictured right; *schloesser-schleissheim.de; combined ticket for three chateaux adult/concession €10/8*). This pompous pile was dreamed up by Prince-Elector Max Emanuel in 1701 in anticipation of his promotion to emperor. It never came. Instead he was forced into exile for over a decade and didn't return to the building until 1715. Cash-flow problems required the scaling back of the original plans, but given the palace's huge dimensions and opulent interior, it's hard to imagine where exactly the cuts fell.

Some of the finest artists of the baroque era were called in to create such eye-pleasing sights as the ceremonial staircase, the Victory Hall and the Grand Gallery. There are outstanding pieces of period furniture, including the elector's four-poster bed, intricately inlaid tables, and a particularly impressive ceiling fresco by Cosmas Damian Asam.

The palace is home to the **Staatsgalerie** (State Gallery), a selection of European baroque art including works by such masters as Peter Paul Rubens, Anthony van Dyck and Carlo Saraceni.

Schloss Lustheim & Altes Schloss Schleissheim

While construction of Neues Schloss Schleissheim was going on, the elector and his retinue resided in the fanciful hunting palace of **Schloss Lustheim**,

© BAYERISCHE SCHLÖSSERVERWALTUNG, MARIA SCHERF U ANDREA GRUBER, WWW.SCHLOESSER.BAYERN.DE

on a little island in the eastern Schlosspark. It now provides an elegant setting for 2000 porcelain masterpieces from Meissen.

The **Altes Schloss Schleissheim** is a mere shadow of its Renaissance self, having been altered and refashioned in the intervening centuries. It houses paintings and sculpture depicting religious culture and festivals all over the world, including a collection of more than 100 nativity scenes.

Flugwerft Schleissheim

The **Flugwerft Schleissheim** *(deutsches-museum .de; adult/child €8/5)*, the aviation branch of the Deutsches Museum, makes for a nice change of pace and aesthetics from the palaces. The 70 historic aircraft, helicopters and gliders exhibited in a vast hangar measuring over 8000 sq metres are fascinating for young visitors in particular and there are lots of hands-on attractions.

QUICK BREAK
The **Schlosswirtschaft Oberschleißheim** near the Altes Schloss is a lovely spot to enjoy lunch or just a post-tour Helles. There is also a pretty beer garden.

★ WORTH A TRIP

Schloss Neuschwanstein

Ludwig II's fairy-tale Schloss Neuschwanstein is Bavaria's most-visited attraction, and as it comes into view for the first time, it is instantly obvious why. This is the Schloss of Disney inspiration, the castle that kids might draw. Some have described it as the world's best.

GETTING THERE
From Munich's Hauptbahnhof, first take the train to Weilheim then board bus 9311 to the castles. The journey takes around 2½ hours. Otherwise take any train to Füssen and take a local bus from there or walk (4km).

Scan for full opening hours and to book ahead.

Schloss Neuschwanstein

Neuschwanstein (pictured right; *neuschwanstein.de; ticket for both castles adult/child €48.50/17*) was built as a romantic medieval fortress: work started in 1869 and, like so many of Ludwig II's grand schemes, was never finished. For all the coffer-splitting sums lavished on it, the king spent just over 170 days in residence.

The most impressive room is the Sängersaal (Minstrels' Hall), whose frescos depict scenes from the opera *Tannhäuser*. Don't miss Ludwig's Tristan and Isolde–themed bedroom, dominated by a huge Gothic-style bed crowned with an intricately carved cathedral-like spire, and the grotto, with more references to *Tannhäuser*. The Byzantine-style Thronsaal (Throne Room) boasts an incredible mosaic floor containing over two million stones. The tour ends with an interesting 20-minute film before you're unleashed into the gift shop.

Schloss Hohenschwangau

You get two for your money here and the 'other' castle is just as interesting. King Ludwig II grew up at **Schloss Hohenschwangau** and later enjoyed long summers here until his death in 1886. It was converted into a summer residence by Ludwig's father Maximilian II on the site of a 12th-century fortress. Far less ostentatious, this castle was actually inhabited for long periods of time. A swan theme runs throughout.

© BAYERISCHE SCHLÖSSERVERWALTUNG, WESTANSICHT, WWW.KREATIV-INSTINKT.DE, WWW.SCHLOESSER.BAYERN.DE

Museum der Bayerischen Könige

There's another attraction here that's well worth seeing before you go – the **Museum der Bayerischen Könige** *(hohenschwangau.de/museum-der-bayerischen-koenige; adult/child €17/2.50)*. Be sure to pick up the detailed audioguide with your ticket.

Opened in 2011, this architecturally impressive building tells the story of the Wittelsbach dynasty. Naturally the focus is skewed towards those who had the greatest influence on the location in which the museum is situated – Maximilian II and his son, King Ludwig II. A highlight of the blingy exhibition includes Ludwig II's famous blue-and-gold robe.

The museum's huge windows provide impressive views of the Alpsee, one of the many lakes to be found around Füssen.

QUICK BREAK
There are several eateries of varying levels of quality around the ticket office at the castles, but basic Alpine-style **Kainz Restaurant** is arguably the best of the bunch.

See p112 for eating, drinking and shopping listings

Explore
Haidhausen, Lehel & Au

Adjoining the Altstadt to the east and straddling the River Isar, Haidhausen, Lehel and Au form a laid-back and quite eclectic area that's great for aimless wandering. While Haidhausen is mostly residential and quite light on sights, Lehel has the second-highest concentration of museums after Maxvorstadt, and Au has a decidedly bucolic, small-town feel. Wedged between Haidhausen and Lehel on an island in the Isar is one of Munich's biggest must-sees, the Deutsches Museum, essential viewing for young and old. When hunger strikes, there are excellent eating options in these parts, mostly without the tourist crush of the Altstadt and offering heaps of neighbourhood flavour.

Getting Around

 U-Bahn
Lehel has a dedicated stop of the same name on the U4 and U5. The nearest stop to the Deutsches Museum is Fraunhoferstrasse on the U1, U2, U7 and U8. Kolumbusplatz in Au is on the same lines.

 Tram
Tram 18 stops at Mariahilfplatz in Au, the Deutsches Museum has its own dedicated stop served by trams 17, 19 and 21, while there is a tram stop in Lehel where the 16 stops.

 **S-Bahn**
Rosenheimerplatz and Ostbahnhof stations are served by many S-Bahn lines.

THE BEST

SCIENCE IN ACTION
Deutsches Museum (p104)

ART NOUVEAU SPLENDOUR
Museum Villa Stuck (p106)

LOST CULTURE
Sudetendeutsches Museum (p107)

TRADITIONAL BEER HALL
Hofbräukeller (p113)

SWIM IN STYLE Müller'sches Volksbad (p109)

Deutsches Museum (p104)
REINHARD KRAUSE/DEUTSCHES MUSEUM

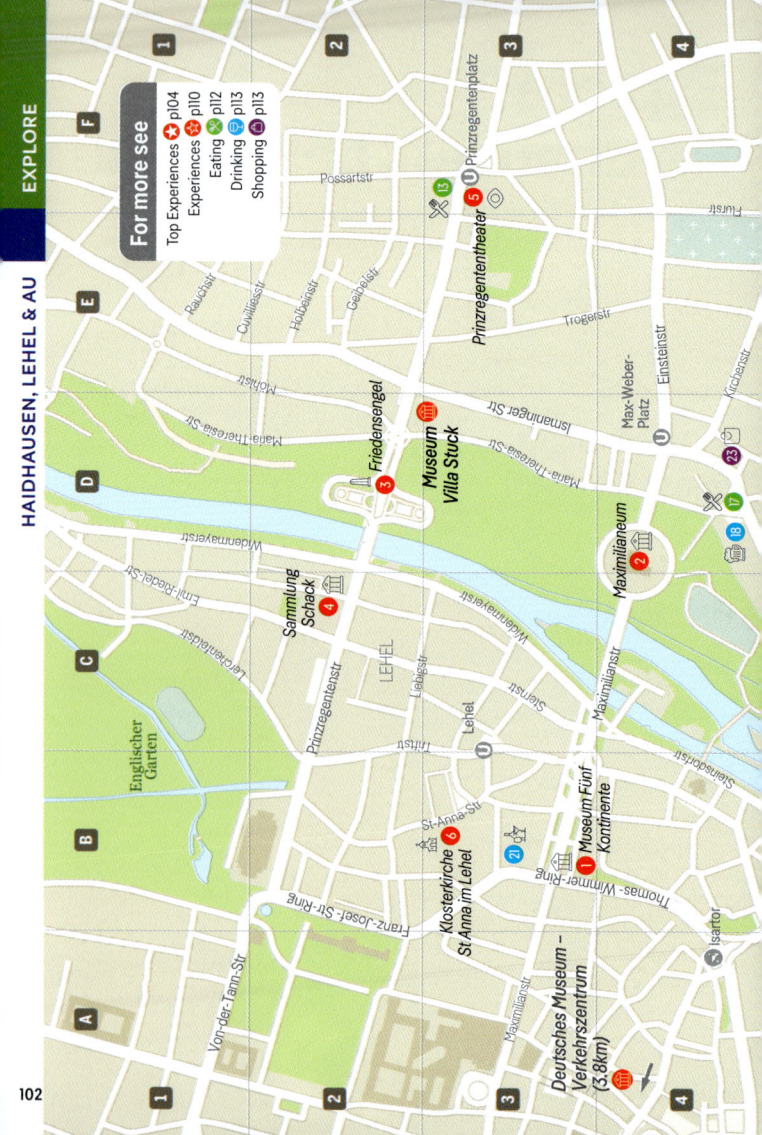

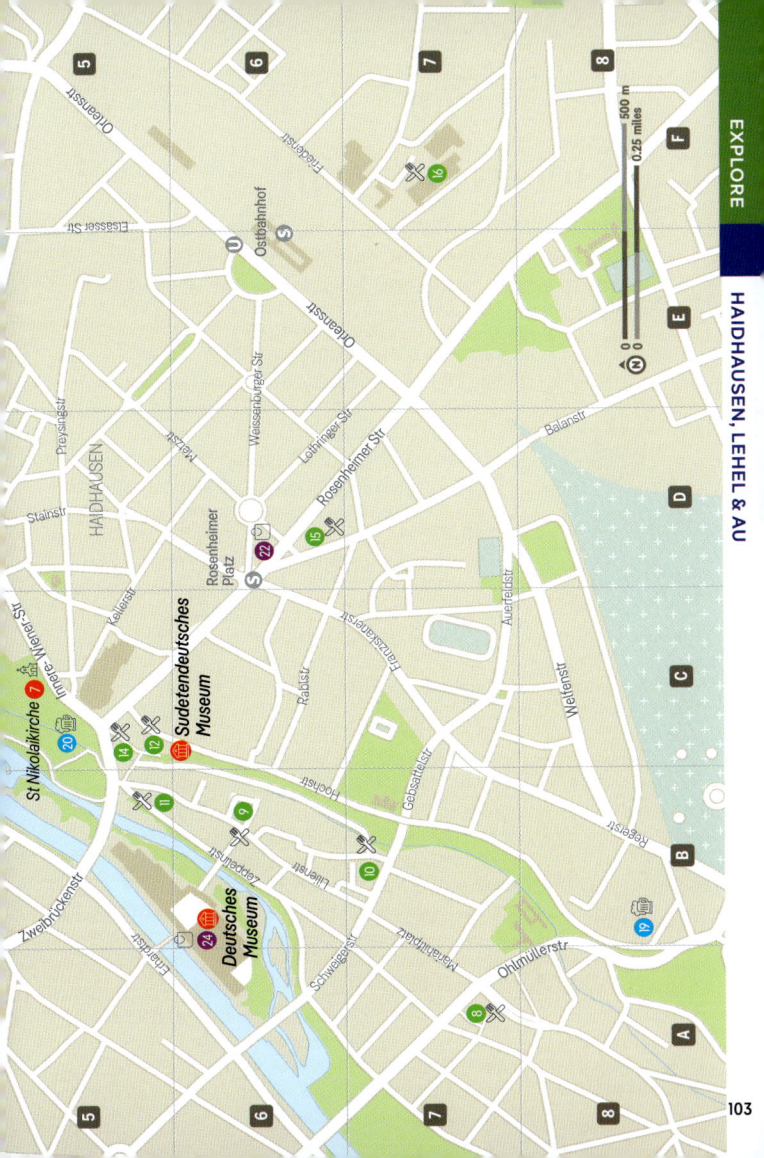

⭐ TOP EXPERIENCE

Deutsches Museum

Even if science isn't usually your thing, a visit to the Deutsches Museum might just show you that physics and engineering are more fun than you thought. This is also one of the best attractions for children of all ages.

MAP P102 **B6**

PLANNING TIP
Save time by purchasing tickets online through the museum website. Even in early spring, the ticket queues are round the building by lunchtime.

Scan for online ticketing and comprehensive information on the Deutsches Museum.

Museum on an Island

The **Deutsches Museum** *(deutsches-museum.de; adult/child €15/8)* fills the Isar's Museumsinsel (Museum Island) almost to capacity, with its hands-on and hands-off exhibitions that explore the worlds of physics, geology, engineering, space travel, aviation and more in surprising detail. Spending a few hours in this temple to technology is an eye-opening journey of discovery, and the exhibitions and demonstrations will certainly be a hit with young, sponge-like minds.

This is a huge museum by any standards; its permanent and temporary exhibitions take up an overwhelming 20,000 sq metres of Munich real estate. A great way to tackle the place is to download the museum app, which will guide you through the highlights in around two hours. There are 20 permanent exhibitions here examining everything from robotics and aviation to healthcare, agriculture and photography. Some of the most memorable exhibits are the complete planes hanging from the ceiling, the U2 rocket that extends for several floors through the building and the 'that's-been-to-the-moon!' space exhibition.

Kinderreich

The place to entertain children aged three to eight is the fabulous Kinderreich, where 1000 activities await, from a child-sized mouse wheel to interactive water fun. Get the kids to climb all over a fire

REINHARD KRAUSE/DEUTSCHES MUSEUM

engine, build things with giant Lego, construct a waterway with canals and locks, or bang on a drum in a – thankfully – soundproof instrument room.

Transport Branch

The **Deutsches Museum – Verkehrszentrum** (*Transport Museum; deutsches-museum.de/verkehrszentrum; adult/child €8/5*) is located on a piece of raised land above the Theresienwiese. An ode to the Bavarian obsession with getting around, this museum explores the ingenious ways humans have devised to transport things and themselves. From the earliest automobiles to famous race cars and high-speed ICE trains, the collection is a virtual trip through transport history. The exhibition is spread over three historic trade-fair halls.

**QUICK BREAK
Cafe Exponat** (p113) in the museum shop is the best option for a coffee or a bite to eat. The museum also has a dedicated picnic area.

★ **TOP EXPERIENCE**

Museum Villa Stuck

Built in 1898 by painter Franz von Stuck, the Villa Stuck provides an enoyable blend of art, architecture and history. The building showcases Munich's Jugendstil (Art Nouveau) design and art. Today, it serves as a museum that honours Stuck's legacy and hosts exhibitions of usually contemporary art.

MAP P102 **D3**

PLANNING TIP
Combine a visit to Villa Stuck with a stroll along nearby Prinzregentenstrasse where you'll find the Friedensengel and the Bavarian National Museum.

Celebrate Art Nouveau at Villa Stuck

The **Museum Villa Stuck** *(villastuck.de; free)* is a must for disciples of the Art Nouveau style. In Germany, this period of art and design is called Jugendstil, and you won't find a better example of a home in this style than the house that once belonged to Franz von Stuck, a leading light in Munich's art scene at the turn of the 20th century and co-founder of the Munich Secession. The exterior of the building sports neoclassical lines, but inside von Stuck went to town using the motifs and materials of the day. The artist even won a gold medal at the legendary 1900 Paris World Exposition, making him one of the most celebrated exponents of the Art Nouveau style in all of Europe. Today this exquisite space is an attraction in itself but also functions as a gallery that hosts changing exhibitions.

Scan this QR code for full opening hours and other information on Villa Stuck.

Villa Revamp

The Villa Stuck reopened after a €14-million renovation in October 2025, which made the building barrier-free and installed technology to protect the fabric of the structure and the art inside.

⭐ TOP EXPERIENCE

Sudetendeutsches Museum

This may be a museum on a niche topic, but the Sudeten German Museum is one of the best-curated museums in Munich and focuses on a chapter in 20th-century history that few are aware of. It's a large institution, reflecting the significance of the Sudeten Germans' contribution to postwar Bavaria.

MAP P102 **C6**

A Lost European Culture

The excellent **Sudetendeutsches Museum** (sudetendeutsches-museum.de; adult/child €5/free) is dedicated to the three million Germans ousted from Bohemia and Moravia at the end of WWII. Large and modern, the four floors of exhibits trace the history of the Sudeten Germans, from their arrival in Bohemia as miners and glassmakers to their radicalisation under Henlein and Hitler and their ultimate mass expulsion from their homes in 1945.

Fate of a People

The museum also examines what became of the Sudeten German culture in Bavaria, where the vast majority ended up, some of them making a significant contribution to the economic miracle decades of the Federal Republic. Some of the exhibitions deal with the traditional industries the Sudeten Germans developed – glass, woodcrafts, jewellery, lace, porcelain, beads etc – many of which the Czechs now call their own. The most moving section is a tumble of actual objects individuals took with them on the transports out of Bohemia and Moravia in 1945. The last floor is all about the life of the one million Sudeten Germans in Bavaria after WWII. Many of them kept the keys to their houses in the hope of a swift return.

QUICK BREAK
There is no eatery on the premises but the parkland to the south is a nice spot by the River Isar for a picnic.

Scan for full opening hours and other information on the Sudetendeutches Museum.

WALKING TOUR

Walk Haidhausen & Au

There's a bit of everything on this leisurely stroll through Haidhausen and Au – from beer gardens to Alpine chalets, a chance to swim and gourmet snacks. The route takes you through spots many tourists go, giving an insight into ordinary neighbourhood life and, if lucky, some lesser-known celebrations.

START	END	LENGTH
Paulaner am Nockherberg	Haidhausen Cemetery	3.4km, two hours

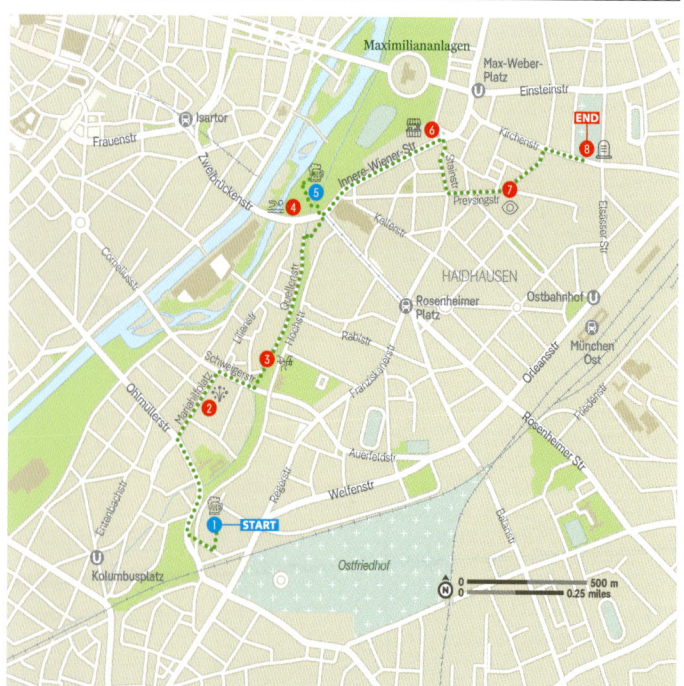

1 Paulaner Brewery

One of Munich's big six breweries, this beer hall and garden has a modern feel and is a refreshing change from the traditional set-up. The **Paulaner am Nockherberg** (p113) comes into its own during Starkbierzeit (February/March) when it serves as a major venue for the festival.

2 Mariahilfplatz

Dominated by the red-brick Mariahilfkirche, **Mariahilfplatz** is the venue for some of Munich's Dult festivals which see the entire expanse fill with traditional stalls, rides and other attractions.

3 Mill Stream

The fast-moving **Auer Mühlbach** once powered mills – hence the name meaning Mill Stream. You can follow it to the next stop through leafy, almost rurally suburban residential areas, one on an island. It's hard to imagine here that you are still essentially in the Munich city centre.

4 Art Nouveau Swimming Pool

Müller'sches Volksbad is an exquisite Art Nouveau affair that first opened its doors in 1901. It's one of Europe's most attractive swimming baths and a dip here under the ornate stuccoed ceiling is a real treat. Despite the period look, it boasts a 21st-century pool and sauna.

5 Muffatwerk Beer Garden

The **Biergarten Muffatwerk** (p113) is a cooler version of the traditional Munich beer garden: reggae instead of oompah, vegetarian plates instead of pig-knuckle platters. There's regular live music in the evenings and a great vibe all day.

6 Gourmet Market

So called as it marked the start of the road to Vienna, busy **Wiener Platz** is known for its daily gourmet market, which has been held since 1901 under a supersized maypole. Tiny cafes and kiosks sell everything from fish mains to chocolate to sausages, and it's a great place to lunch or snack.

7 17th-century Home

In Preysingstrasse, the conspicuously old, all-timber **Kriechbaumhof** looks like it's been teleported from the Alps. It dates back to the 17th century and is the last residential building from the period left standing in Munich. Currently housing the youth wing of the German Alpine Club, it is slated for much-needed renovation in coming years.

8 Haidhausen Cemetery

The austere, slender spire of the Church of John the Baptist rises above Kirchenstrasse. The adjoining and somewhat overgrown walled **cemetery**, one of Munich's most attractive, has elaborate tombs in different artistic styles.

EXPERIENCES

Explore Five Continents at Fünf Kontinente
ETHNOGRAPHIC MUSEUM

MAP: ① P102 B3

One of Munich's least-visited collections (despite the attractive €1 Sunday admission) must be the **Museum Fünf Kontinente** (*Five Continents Museum; museum-fuenf-kontinente.de; adult/child €5/free, Sun €1*), which is housed in a palace located on thundering Maximilianstrasse. The collections are made up of art and artefacts brought from across the globe by various expeditions. The initial rooms focus heavily on Myanmar before moving on to Thai Buddhas, buildings of the Islamic world, masks from Oceania, Peruvian costumes, North American headdresses and much more. As ethnographical collections go, it's pretty good, but the museum lacks a bit of oomph and innovation. And in case you were wondering, the two missing continents are Europe and Antarctica.

Climb up to the Maximilianeum
HISTORIC BUILDING

MAP: ② P102 D4

Maximilianstrasse culminates in the glorious **Maximilianeum**, completed in 1874, a decade after Maximilian II's sudden death. It's an imposing structure, drawn like a theatre curtain across a hilltop, bedecked with mosaics, paintings and other artistic objects. It's framed by an undulating park called the Maximiliananlagen, which is a haven for cyclists in summer and tobogganists in winter. This imposing structure isn't just a pretty ornament – the **Bavarian State Parliament** sits inside.

One interesting fact about the Maximilianeum is that six to eight students live for free in the building – it was originally set up as an educational foundation for gifted youngsters.

Look up to Munich's Angel of Peace
STATUE

MAP: ③ P102 D2

North across the Maximiliananlagen rises the **Friedensengel**, aka the Angel of Peace, that was erected atop a 23m-tall column to mark 25 years of peace after the Franco-German War of 1870–71. Lined up with Prinzregentenstrasse as it crosses the River Isar via the Luitpold Bridge, the gilt, winged figure creates a photogenic spectacle.

Visit Count Schack
ART MUSEUM

MAP: ④ P102 C2

Count Adolf Friedrich von Schack (1815–94) was a great fan of 19th-century Romantic painters such as Böcklin, Feuerbach and von Schwind. His collection is housed in the former Prussian embassy, now the **Sammlung Schack** (*pinakothek.de; adult/concession €4/3*). A tour of the intimate space is like an escape into the idealised fantasy worlds created by these artists.

Admire a Munich Theatre for Wagner   GRAND THEATRE
MAP: ❺ P102 **F3**

One of the area's main architectural landmarks is the **Prinzregententheater** *(theaterakademie.de),* a typically grand piece of 19th-century public architecture. Its dramatic mix of Art Nouveau and neoclassical styles was conceived under Prince Regent Luitpold as a festival house for Richard Wagner operas. The theatre opened in 1901 with a performance of Wagner's *Die Meistersinger von Nürnberg.* Today it is home to the Bavarian Theatre Academy, which celebrated its 30th birthday in 2023. Performances here range from Beethoven and chamber orchestras to farces and musicals. Wagner is nowhere to be seen on the programme.

Peek into the Klosterkirche St Anna im Lehel   HISTORIC CHURCH
MAP: ❻ P102 **B3**

The Asamkirche may be more sumptuous, but the **Klosterkirche St Anna im Lehel** is actually a collaboration of the top dogs of the rococo. Johann Michael Fischer designed the building and Cosmas Damian Asam painted the stunning ceiling fresco and altar. This was the first rococo church to be built in Munich.

Visit St Nick   HISTORIC CHURCH
MAP: ❼ P102 **C5**

Sitting back from thundering Rosenheimer Strasse, the **St Nikolaikirche** was first built in 1315 in Gothic style, only to go all baroque three centuries later. Outside the prim church ensemble of St Nikolai and Lorettokapelle, the covered walkway protects some pretty 'Stations of the Cross' made using Nymphenburg porcelain.

CYCLING MUNICH

Munich is one of the world's best cities for sightseeing with your feet on pedals. And the good news is you don't have to haul your two-wheeler to Bavaria, nor know where you are going – there are plenty of pedalling enthusiasts here to help you with both. **Radius Tours & Bike Rental** *(radiustours.com)* is a Munich original that has been around for years, hiring bikes and running tours for tens of thousands of visitors since the 1980s. Its Munich Bike Tour is still the best. Another reliable and longstanding operator is **Mike's Bike Tours** *(mikesbiketours.com),* which runs organised bike tours of Munich and offers bike rental.

LISTINGS

Best Places for...

€ Budget €€ Midrange €€€ Top End

Eating

Bavarian Favourites

Schoberwirt €

8 A7

This classic, understated and conservative tavern claims to be staunchly Bavarian, though the odd bit of tuna and lemon make it onto the menu. The venison goulash, cheese *Spätzle* and many other folksy dishes are very reasonably priced. *5-11.30pm Wed & Thu, 10.30am-midnight Fri-Sun*

Wirtshaus in der Au €€

9 B6

This is arguably Haidhausen's best neighbourhood resto-pub, with a convivial atmosphere, beer-and-dumpling philosophy and English-language Knödel-centric cookery courses. Crackling fireplace in winter but this is sadly only open in the evenings. *5-11pm Mon-Fri, from 10am Sat & Sun*

Ayinger in der Au €€

10 B7

Staunchly traditional, largely tourist-free Bavarian restaurant and beer venue next to the Auer Mühlbach serving a seasonally influenced menu, *Weisswurst* breakfasts and Sunday brunches. *5-11.30pm Wed & Thu, 10.30am-midnight Fri-Sun*

Gourmet Finery

Showroom €€

11 B5

A Michelin star twinkles brightly at this long-standing, gourmet haven where the six- to eight-course menu changes every two weeks and the cooking is highly innovative. *6pm-1am Mon-Fri*

Exotic Eats

Bohemia München €

12 C5

Located somewhat ironically behind the Sudetendeutsches Museum, this Czech restaurant specialises in the hearty cooking of Bavaria's neighbour. Expect lots of dumplings, pork, sauerkraut and beer. *noon-10pm Wed-Sun*

Swagat €€

13 F3

Long-established Swagat fills an intimate cellar space with Indian fabrics and cavorting Hindu gods. There is plenty to please noncarnivores. *11.30am-2.30pm & 5.30pm-1am*

Chopan – Gasteig €€

14 C5

This branch of Chopan, the incredibly successful mini-chain of Afghan restaurants in Munich, is low-lit in design, with rice dishes, grilled meat, salads and lentils populating the menu. *5-11pm*

Der Sizilianer €€

15 D6

There seems to be a generic 'Italian' restaurant on every street these days in Munich, so it is refreshing to find an eatery focusing on a single Italian cuisine: very authentic Sicilian. Expect lots of lemon, polenta, arancini and full-bodied wines. *8am-4pm Mon-Fri*

See p102 for map of locations

Cafes & Light Bites

Cafe Exponat €
see B6

A solid option within the Deutsches Museum complex if you're after a sandwich between exhibitions. Its next to the museum shop. *10am-4pm*

Werksviertel €€
 F7

The Werksviertel is a modern neighbourhood built south of the Ostbahnhof in recent decades and one that boasts a high concentration of exotic street and fast-food joints. There's Thai, Vietnamese, Mexican, Ukrainian and many others. *hours vary*

Fischhäusl €€
 D4

This Wiener Platz kiosk with a few seats is one of the best spots in Munich to lunch on fish. The fried fish in a bun is a cheap and filling lunch. *9.30am-6pm Tue-Fri, 9am-2.30pm Sat*

Drinking

All about the Beer

Hofbräukeller
 D4

At the Wiener Platz, this is a Munich original beer hall with a wood-panelled dining room and Hofbräu on tap. Behind the building is what many regard as Munich's first beer garden (though the title is also claimed by others). *10am-midnight*

Paulaner am Nockherberg
 B8

Off the beaten tourist trail in Au, the modern restaurant and beer garden at the Paulaner brewery is a lively option from lunch till late. Slightly more upmarket feel and less noisy ambience. *noon-midnight*

Biergarten Muffatwerk
 C5

A welcome (by some) alternative to the pork knuckle and *Weisswurst* of the tourist hotspots, this 400-seater beer garden at the Muffatwerk Arts Centre has a menu of healthier food but the same beer as elsewhere. Only open in good weather. *noon-late*

Bars

Hermanns
 B3

Stylish bar-resto where the wine, champagne and light Italian cuisine sit well with the plush, red-velvet interior and uniformed waiting staff. One of Munich's best drinks and cocktail menus. *11.30am-late Tue-Fri, to 4pm Mon, 6pm-1am Sat*

Shopping

Vintage Finds

Vintage Etcetera
 D6

Vintage clothes as well as traditional Dirndl come Oktoberfest time, plus preloved jewellery and other small knickknacks. *10am-6pm Mon-Fri, to 2pm Sat*

Macy
23 D4

Great secondhand shop on Johannisplatz for the discerning purchaser of fine used clothing. Every piece is a treasure unearthed. *11am-7pm Mon-Fri, to 4pm Sat*

Museum Shops

Deutsches Museum Shop
24 B6

One of Munich's best museum shops with experiments, toys, puzzles and thought-provoking merch galore. *9am-5pm*

See p132 for eating and drinking listings

Explore
Nymphenburg, BMW & Olympiapark

Occupying a huge swath of northwest Munich, the neighbourhoods of Nymphenburg, Neuhausen and the Olympiapark are a varied trio. The Olympiapark is mostly about one thing – the venues left over from the 1972 summer Olympics. Nymphenburg is all about its royal palace, Munich's finest, while mostly residential Neuhausen has Europe's largest beer garden.

And if you didn't know, Bavaria makes some pretty good cars – BMW is based right next to the Olympiapark, with the visitor experience revolving mostly around the free-to-enter BMW World and the company's unsurpassed museum, though factory tours are also possible with preplanning.

Getting Around

 **U-Bahn**
The best stop for the Olympiapark and BMW is Olympiazentrum, served by the U3.

 Tram
The only way to reach Nymphenburg by public transport is aboard tram 17, alighting at the Schloss Nymphenburg stop. Trams 20 and 21 run to Olympiapark West.

 **S-Bahn**
The Hirschgarten beer garden is a short walk from both the Laim and Hirschgarten S-Bahn.

 Bus
Bus 144 cuts through the Olympiapark on its way between Scheidplatz and Rotkreuzplatz U-Bahn stations.

Schloss Nymphenburg (p127)
© BAYERISCHE SCHLÖSSERVERWALTUNG, GROSSES PARTERRE,
WWW.SCHLOESSER.BAYERN.DE

THE BEST

AUTOMOTIVE HISTORY
BMW Museum (p124)

ROYAL GRANDEUR Schloss Nymphenburg (p127)

MUNICH VIEWS
Olympiaturm (p118)

EXTRA-LARGE BEER GARDEN
Hirschgarten (p133)

MOTORING PROWESS
BMW Welt (p123)

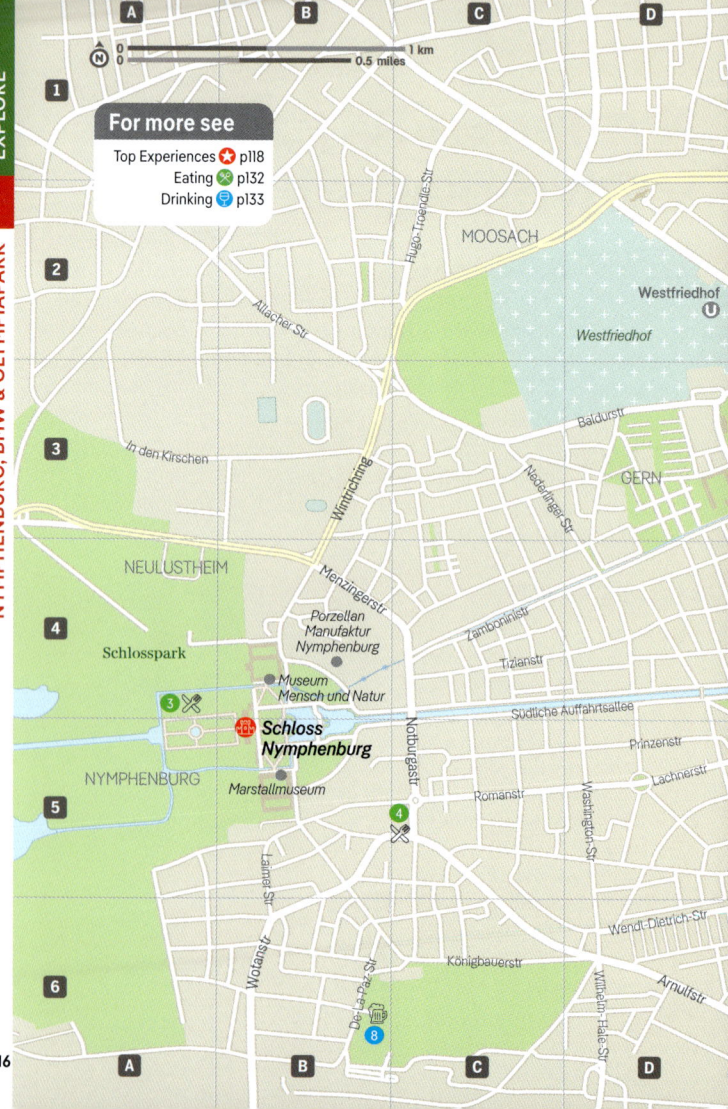

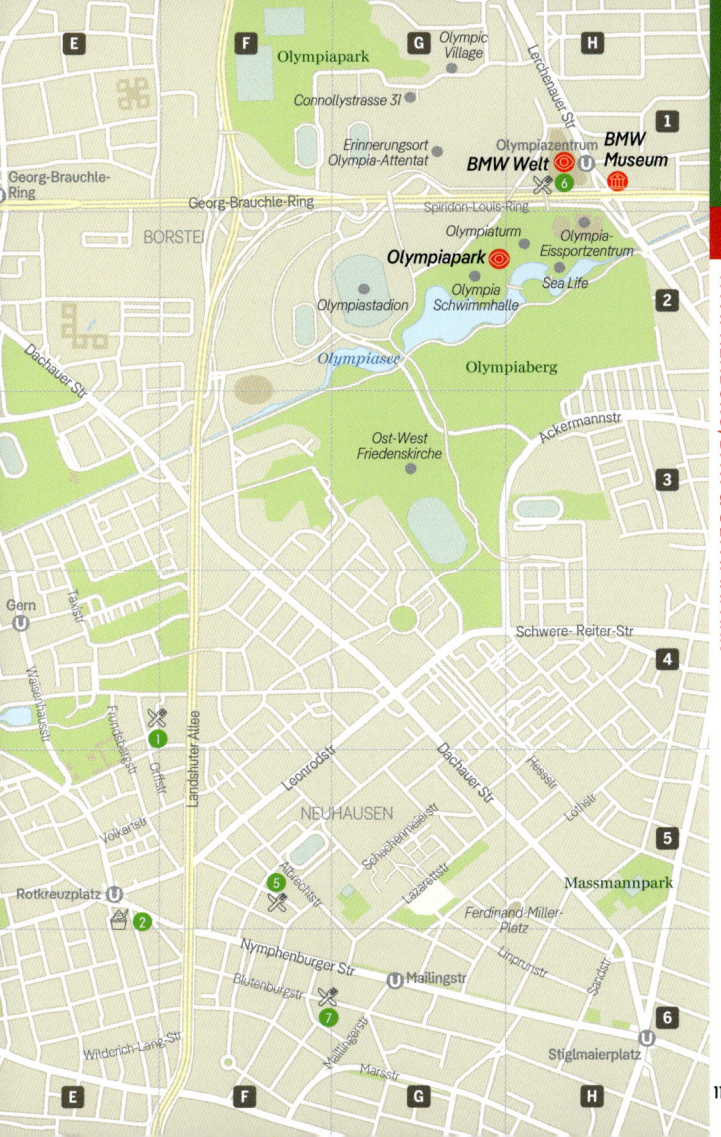

★ TOP EXPERIENCE

Olympiapark

The 1972 summer Olympics were significant for Munich as they gave the city a chance to make a break with the past. It was the first time the country had hosted the games since the 1936 Berlin Olympics. The Olympiapark was begun in the late 1960s.

MAP P116 **G2**

PLANNING TIP
The Olympiapark is largely an outdoor experience with sometimes relatively long walks between attractions. Check the weather forecast before you set off.

Scan for all the information you could ever need on visiting the Olympiapark.

Olympiastadion

With its contorted steel and Plexiglass tent roof, which stretches across the stands, the **Olympiastadion** was the dazzling centrepiece for the Munich Olympics and remains an instantly recognisable structure, especially for football fans – Bayern Munich played here until 2006 (when they moved to the equally impressive Allianz Arena) and West Germany famously won the 1974 FIFA World Cup on this hallowed turf. The phenomenal stadium must have seemed like the work of alien beings in 1972. In recent times there were daredevil tours of the roof, and the stadium was regularly used for sports and live music events including concerts by some of the world's biggest stars. In 2025 the stadium closed for renovation work, evidently in preparation for the Olympic bid.

Olympiaturm

The top visitor attraction at the Olympiapark is the 290m-tall **Olympiaturm** *(adult/child €13/10)*. The tower's lift to the three-level viewing platform 190m above ground is so fast that your stomach arrives several seconds after you do! You'll be rewarded with the best views of Munich bar none. The Alps are clearly visible when climatic conditions play ball. There's a cafe here and Munich's highest geocache as well as various exhibitions on the future of the Olympiapark. If you only have time to visit one attraction here, this should be it.

Olympiaberg

A short walk to the south of the tower on the other side of the Olympiasee lake, the **Olympiaberg** (Olympic Mountain) rises 60m into the air (the top is at an altitude of 565m above sea level) and affords views of the park, the BMW complex, much of the city and sometimes the Alps. Incredibly, the 'mountain' was created from the WWII air raid rubble from the city centre in the late 1940s and predates even the idea of holding the Olympics here. Its slopes have witnessed winter sports championships including snowboarding and slalom events.

QUICK BREAK
There are surprisingly few places to eat in the Olympiapark so bring a picnic to enjoy on the wide lawns or at the top of the Olympiaberg.

VIACHESLAV LOPATIN/SHUTTERSTOCK

YASEMIN OZDEMIR/SHUTTERSTOCK

1972 Games Venues

Renovated a couple of times since the 1972 Games, the indoor **Olympia Schwimmhalle** (Olympic Swimming Hall; pictured above) is the most modern and well-equipped swimming complex in Munich. When there isn't an event on it operates as a public swimming pool. The **Olympia-Eissportzentrum** (Olympic Ice Sports Centre) was actually the first sports facility to open here in 1967. It hosted boxing during the Games but for most of its life served as an ice rink and ice-hockey stadium. In 2025, the complex began another transformation, this time into an action sports centre for skateboarding, BMX and parkour. It is likely to be closed until 2030 and will feature prominently in any future Munich bid for a summer Olympics.

OLYMPICS RECYCLED?

Munich plans to bid for the 2036, 2040 or 2044 summer games, and, in an Olympic first, recycle the 1972 venue for the event. It would perfectly combine the locals' passion for sport and reusing stuff.

Ost-West Friedenskirche

One of the most intriguing sights at the Olympiapark has nothing to do with the 1972 Games and predates the complex by two decades. Built illegally after WWII by Russian hermit Father Timofey and his wife using debris from what would become the Olympiaberg, the delightfully rural Orthodox **Ost-West Friedenskirche** (East-West Peace Church) was to have been demolished for the 1972 Olympic Games but protests led to the repositioning of some of the venues further north. When Timofey died in 2004 his adjacent house was made into a museum dedicated to his life, work and the church.

The buildings were two of only a handful of structures within the Olympiapark that predated the Games, but in June 2023 the church burnt down. It's thought the authorities are likely to have it rebuilt as a symbol of peace in the city, though no definite plans exist as yet. Although the site of the church is now just an empty plot, the small piece of woodland still contains the wonderful museum.

Remembering a Tragedy

The 1972 Olympics are unfortunately known for the attack carried out by Palestinian terrorists during which Israeli athletes were kidnapped and killed. The surprisingly recent (2017) **Erinnerungsort Olympia-Attentat** memorial, just to the south of the Olympic village, remembers the victims. Housed beneath a striking wedge of concrete, a 10-minute video plays on a constant loop, relating the events of those terrible days with period footage. The life stories of the victims are posted opposite – some survived Nazi concentration camps only to die at the hands of terrorists in Germany. The hostages were taken within the Olympic village at **Connollystrasse 31**, a five-minute walk from the memorial, where there is a plaque in German and Hebrew. Continue along Connollystrasse to see the rest of the **Olympic village** where some sections

WALK OF FAME
Check out Munich's very own walk of fame on the north side of the Olympiasee with handprints left by some of the biggest names in pop, rock and sport. Boris Becker, Kylie Minogue, Cliff Richard, Meat Loaf and Bryan Ferry are just some of the performers at the Olympiastadion to have pressed their hands into wet concrete here.

MCMILAN/SHUTTERSTOCK

AUDIOGUIDE
There are lots of tours available but if you just want to go at your own pace, the Olympiapark audioguide does a superb job of taking you around the complex.

remain in a 1970s time warp, especially the part around the shopping precinct where there are some cheap eateries and a supermarket.

Sea Life

Added decades after the Games ended, **Sea Life** (*visitsealife.com; adult/child €22/17.50*) is one of Munich's top attractions for families with children. Reef sharks, moray eels and seahorses are among the thousands of creatures on display in monster aquariums which are divided into geographical locations, including Munich's own River Isar, which actually contains some surprisingly large inhabitants.

⭐ TOP EXPERIENCE

The BMW Experience

Munich is the home of BMW (Bayerische Motoren Werke), possibly the biggest brand name ever to emerge from the Free State. The factory is located right next door to the Olympiapark on the Petuelring and this is where you'll also find BMW Welt and the BMW Museum.

MAP P116 **H1**

Headquarters of a Legend

Situated high above the thundering intersection of Petuelring and Lerchenauer Strasse, the BMW Tower rises like four engine pistons poised to fire. The headquarters of BMW, the tower was completed just in time for the 1972 Olympics next door, a sly bit of stealth advertising! Both the tower and the museum below are the work of Austrian architect Karl Schwanzer.

The World of BMW

Even if you aren't into tomorrow's e-mobiles or spoiler design for the latest M3, BMW World is still well worth a look, if only to enviously admire southern Germany's engineering prowess. Most start at **BMW Welt** (BMW World; bmw-welt.com), a free exhibition, showroom and experience all rolled into one.

The first thing you notice when emerging from the Olympiazentrum U-Bahn station is the building's striking, statement architecture, especially the double cone (the work of Coop Himmelb(l)au Architects) like a tornado spiralling down from a dark cloud the size of an aircraft carrier. Inside, the exhibitions showcase the best of BMW's current output as well as acting as a big branding exercise and as

PLANNING TIP
Many visitors combine the indoor pleasures of BMW with lawn time across at the Olympiapark in a single day out. The BMW attractions are also ideal for rainy days.

Scan for tickets, opening hours and to book guided tours.

BMW AG

1972 E-MOBILE
BMW supplied vehicles to the 1972 Olympic organising committee – believe it or not an electric car with a whopping 30km range. You'll see it in the museum.

a facility for handing over the keys to proud new owners (for a hefty fee). Straddle powerful motor-bikes, marvel at technology-packed e-saloons and estates (no tyre kicking, please) or learn more about the technology that goes into BMW's cars. There are guided tours, a couple of cafes and robots roaming the floor providing information (there are strategically located humans, too).

If your budget doesn't stretch to a new Rolls Royce Ghost (yes, BMW make those, too), you might at least be in a financial position to buy a branded pencil in the astronomically expensive BMW Welt Lifestyle & Accessory Shop. Otherwise leave via the double cone to reach the museum.

BMW Museum
Linked to BMW Welt by a special space-age foot-bridge, the **BMW Museum** *(adult/child €14/8)* is

another piece of striking architecture, this time a gigantic silver bowl. Inside the exhibition is divided into 22 themed spaces, all brightly illuminated, multi-levelled and conveniently numbered, that take you through the BMW story as well as highlighting significant vehicles, technologies and company activities. Highlights include a monster wall of BMW motorbikes through the ages, a room of old adverts and TV commercials in a tiny cinema, an exhibition dedicated to the iconic 1950s Isetta (which most people erroneously assume only had three wheels; pictured below), a showroom's worth of M series, and Elvis' 507, the car he bought while serving in the US Army in Germany in the late 1950s (see p126).

More thought-provoking parts deal openly with BMW's use of slave labour during the Nazi period

QUICK BREAK
The best place to grab a coffee or a bite to eat is the **Biker's Lodge** which is upstairs by the motorbike exhibition.

ANTON IVANOV/SHUTTERSTOCK

and the company's commitment to sustainable motoring – the section on hydrogen-powered vehicles will certainly grow in future years; watch this space. All in all, it's a fascinating journey, even for those who can't tell a telescopic fork from their axle load distribution. Allow at least two hours to see everything at a canter.

Guided Tours

Hardcore Bayerische Motoren Werke fans might want to take one of the guided tours offered by the staff at both **BMW World** *(adult/concession €16/14)* and the **museum** *(adult/concession €20/12)*. Both take 60 minutes and you should book around three days beforehand for English. Another interesting tour called **BMW Group Classic** *(groups only, adult/concession €19/14)* takes visitors into one of the company's first production halls, now a protected building, where BMW has another secret museum of classic models. All tours can be booked through the website.

BMW Plant Tours

With a bit of forward planning, you can also have a guided tour of the **BMW Plant** *(adult/child €20/18)* which extends beyond the museum. Perhaps only for die-hard BMW fans, this two-hour, 3km stroll takes you behind the scenes of the truly state-of-the-art BMW production facility here and runs in English and German. It is hugely popular with locals and tourists and should be booked in advance through *bmw-welt.com*. Plant tours only run from Monday to Friday. As you are entering a real production facility, there are rules visitors must adhere to during the tour. Participants must understand the language in which the tour is given (German or English) or bring an interpreter. Photography is strictly prohibited. Children must be accompanied by an adult.

LOVE ME FENDER

The story of Elvis' BMW roadster is a real piece of 20th-century legend. The King bought the car in 1958 when serving in the US Army in Germany. He had it shipped home at the end of his service, but later sold it. The car was discovered in a bad state in 2014 and lovingly restored by the BMW Museum.

⭐ TOP EXPERIENCE

Schloss Nymphenburg

Jump aboard tram 17 heading west from the Hauptbahnhof and within 15 minutes you'll find yourself at the gates of Schloss Nymphenburg, for many Munich's most illustrious palace and the Wittelsbach dynasty's summer residence. And when you are done with the tour, there's much else to discover here.

MAP P116 **B5**

Summer with the Wittelsbachs

Set amid generous gardens and placid water features, imperious **Schloss Nymphenburg** (schloss-nymphenburg.de; adult/concession €10/9) lies around 5km northwest of the Altstadt. Begun in 1664 as a villa for Electress Adelaide of Savoy, this royal palace was extended over the next century to become the Wittelsbach family's opulent summer abode we see today. Franz, Duke of Bavaria, head of the Wittelsbach family, still occupies an apartment here.

The main palace building consists of a large villa and two wings of squeaking parquet floors and sumptuous period rooms. The self-guided tour kicks off in the highly decorative, rococo **Festsaal** (Grosser or Steinerner Saal), which dominates the central section of the building. Soon comes the most famous room in the whole Schloss, the **Schönheitengalerie** (Gallery of the Beauties), housed in the former apartments of Queen Caroline. Some 38 portraits of females chosen by an 'admiring' King Ludwig I peer from the walls. The most famous image is of Helene Sedlmayr, the daughter of a shoemaker, wearing a lavish frock the king gave her for the sitting. You'll also find Ludwig's lover Lola Montez, as well as 19th-century

PLANNING TIP
Note that the follies and minipalaces in the grounds of Schloss Nymphenburg are closed between mid-October and 1 April.

Scan for full opening hours and other information.

© BAYERISCHE SCHLÖSSERVERWALTUNG, MARIA SCHERF & VERONIKA FREUDLING, WWW.SCHLOSS-NYMPHENBURG.DE

gossip-column celebrity Lady Jane Ellenborough and English Lady Jane Erskin.

The tour route then visits the **Queen's Bedroom**, which still contains the sleigh bed on which Ludwig II was born, and the **King's Chamber**, resplendent with three-dimensional ceiling frescos. Other notable rooms include **Cuvilliés' Chinese Lacquer Room** and the **baroque chapel**. Allow at least 90 minutes to see everything.

Grounds, Follies & Minipalaces

After the tour of the main palace, you can continue your day at Nymphenburg with a wander around the extensive **grounds** which contain several follies and minipalaces.

The park's chief folly is the **Amalienburg**, a small hunting lodge dripping with crystal and gilt decoration and the work of the Wittelsbachs'

QUICK BREAK
Next to the palace, the **Schlosscafé im Palmenhaus** (p132) is the only place to have a bite to eat and a stylish one at that.

favourite architect, Cuvilliés. Inside don't miss the amazing **Spiegelsaal** (hall of mirrors). The two-storey **Pagodenburg** was built in the early 18th century as a Chinese teahouse and is swathed in ceramic tiles depicting landscapes, figures and floral ornamentation. The **Badenburg** is a sauna and bathing house that still has its original heating system. Finally, the **Magdalenenklause** was built as a mock hermitage in faux-ruined style.

The park is at its most magical without the masses, early in the morning and an hour before closing. But even in the daytime, you can usually commune in solitude with water lilies and singing frogs at the **Kugelweiher pond** in the far northern corner.

Duo of Museums

When you've seen the main palace building and the grounds, Schloss Nymphenburg is also home to two worthwhile museums, one of them being a children's Munich highlight.

The **Marstallmuseum** (pictured left; *adult/concession €8/7*) displays royal coaches and riding gear, including Ludwig II's fairy-tale-like rococo sleigh, ingeniously fitted with oil lamps for his nocturnal outings. Upstairs is the world's largest collection of porcelain, made by the famous Nymphenburger manufacturer. Also known as the Sammlung Bäuml, it presents the entire product palette from the company's founding in 1747 until 1930.

In Nymphenburg's north wing, the **Museum Mensch und Natur** (*Museum of Humankind & Nature; mmn-muenchen.snsb.de; adult/child €3.50/free*) has nothing to do with the royal grandeur of the Schloss, and kids will have plenty of ooh and aah moments here. Anything but old school, it puts a premium on interactive displays, models and audiovisual presentations on themes such as food, the Earth and the human body. It's mostly in German, but few language skills are needed to appreciate the visuals.

ROYAL SOUVENIR
The royal porcelain manufacturer, **Porzellan Manufaktur Nymphenburg**, is based near the palace. Its delicate pieces, often bearing traditional Bavarian motifs, are of the highest quality. If you're in the market for a pricey but beautiful souvenir, head for the company's flagship store on the Nördliches Schlossrondell by the lake as you enter the complex.

Walk Olympiapark

With fresh legs and a sunny day, there are few better places to stroll than the venue for the 1972 summer Olympic Games. The sights included on this route are eclectic to say the least. Sturdy shoes and a picnic may come in handy.

START	END	LENGTH
Olympic Village	Flohmarkt in Olympiapark	4.5km, 2½ hours

1 Olympic Village

The northern exits of the Olympiazentrum U-Bahn station deliver you to the entrances to the 1972 **Olympic village**. The multilevel walkways are a bit of a maze and the whole complex has a very retro feel to it. It's a very interesting place for aimless wandering.

2 Visitor Centre

The multitasking **visitor centre** is a general information and tour meeting point and ticket office for tours as well as events. This should be your first port of call within the park itself, even if it's just to pick up a map.

3 Stop at the Lake

Between the Olympiaberg and the Olympiaturm is the **Olympiasee**, an artificial lake that is more than 1km long and is fed partially from rainwater from the roofs of the Olympic venues. Bathing is not permitted, but you can hire boats on the opposite bank to the tower.

4 Open-air Cinema

The **Kino am Olympiasee** is one of Bavaria's best cinemas with after-dark screenings of English-language films (in English) on most days over the summer. There are also special children's showings while it is still light. Seating is on deckchairs and there are ample refreshments available.

5 Olympia Mountain

It's a bit of a huff and puff up the spiralling paths to the top of the **Olympiaberg** (p119) – at 60m high, it's not much of a 'berg' but the view from the top is worth the effort of getting up there.

6 East-West Peace Church

Just below the Olympiaberg, on wasteland used for parking tour lorries, a copse of trees hides one of Munich's most fascinating little offbeat sights – the erstwhile site of the **Ost-West Friedenskirche** (p121). The small museum here is a delight though the church is no more.

7 Sports Arena

The most recent addition to the Olympiapark and another piece of clever prep for the upcoming Olympic bid, the **SAP Garden** is a state-of-the-art, multipurpose sports arena completed in 2024 that can host ice hockey and basketball matches. EHC München moved here from the Olympia-Eissportzentrum and Bayern Munich basketball team also call this home.

8 Flea Market

What does every German city do with its spare bits of land – why hold a flea market on them, of course! The jumble sale at the **Flohmarkt im Olympiapark** takes place at the huge car park on the western side of the Olympiapark almost every Friday and Saturday morning.

LISTINGS

Best Places for...

€ Budget €€ Midrange €€€ Top End

See p116 for map of locations

Eating

Cafes with History

Ruffini €
1 F4

One of Munich's best cafes with a lot of history is buried deep in Neuhausen but is well worth the effort to find. Light, airy and simple, the focus here is firmly on quality wine, great breakfasts and a convivial vibe. *10am-midnight Tue-Sun*

Eiscafé Sarcletti €
2 E5

Ice-cream fanatics in the know have been flocking to this cafe near Rotkreuzplatz U-Bahn station since 1879 and it is well worth breaking your journey to Nymphenburg to try the mouthwatering creations here. *9am-9pm mid-Feb–mid-Nov*

Schlosscafé im Palmenhaus €€
3 A4

The glass-fronted 1820s palm house where Ludwig II used to keep his exotic house plants warm in winter is now a high-ceilinged and pleasantly scented cafe serving soups, salads, sandwiches and other light meals. It's just behind Schloss Nymphenburg. *11am-6pm Thu-Sun*

Meal at Hirschgarten

REGULA WOLF

Neighbourhood Favourites

Café Romanplat €
4 C5

Much-lauded neighbourhood cafe with big breakfasts, cakes stacked high and some of Munich's best ice cream. *9am-6pm Sun-Fri*

Fine Dining

Zauberberg €€€
5 F5

Far off the tourist track, this gourmet bolt hole is known for its set menus that range from three to six courses. The cooking here is exceptional, a fact recognised with a Michelin review. *6pm-midnight Wed-Sat*

Bavarie by Käfer €€€
6 H1

The newest addition to the BMW-Welt's gastronomic offerings is this upmarket brasserie that does a good line in drinks to enjoy on the terrace and some pricey but well-crafted international dishes, despite the name. *noon-3pm Mon-Sat, 6-10pm Tue-Sat*

Ethnic Treats

Chopan €€
7 G6

This Afghan eatery is a much-lauded restaurant done out in the style of a Central Asian caravanserai, with rich fabrics, multihued glass lanterns and geometric patterns. *6-11pm*

Drinking

Beer Gardens

Hirschgarten
8 B6

The Everest of all beer gardens can seat up to 8700 Augustiner lovers, making it the world's biggest. It's in a lovely spot in a former royal hunting preserve and rubs up against a deer enclosure and a carousel. Steer here after visiting Schloss Nymphenburg – it's only a short walk south of the palace. *11am-midnight*

★ TOP EXPERIENCE

Oktoberfest

The world's largest drink-a-thon and the traditional highlight of Bavaria's events calendar, Oktoberfest is one of the best-known fairs on Earth. No other event manages to mix such a level of crimson-faced humour, drunken debauchery and excessive beer consumption with so much tradition, history… and oompah music.

PLANNING TIP
If there's one thing you need to sort out at least a year before you arrive for Oktoberfest, it's accommodation. Competition for beds is fierce and prices astronomical.

Scan to find out everything you could possibly want to know about Oktoberfest.

A Little History

The world's biggest beer festival has its origins in a simple horse race. In 1810 Bavarian crown prince Ludwig, later King Ludwig I, married Princess Therese of Saxe-Hildburghausen, and following the wedding a horse race was held at the city gates. The six-day celebration was such a galloping success that it became an annual event, was extended and moved forward to start in September so that visitors could enjoy warmer weather and lighter nights. The horse race, which quickly became a sideshow, ended in 1960, but an agricultural show is still part of the Oktoberfest, albeit a minor one.

Ozapft Ist's!

As early as mid-July the brewery crews move in to start erecting the tents which almost fill the Theresienwiese, a gravelly open space in the western reaches of Munich city centre known locally as the Wiesn.

Starting at 10.45am on the first day, the brewer's parade (the Festzug) travels through the city centre from the River Isar to the fairgrounds. This involves many old, brightly decorated horse-drawn carriages once used to transport kegs from brewery

FOOTTOO/SHUTTERSTOCK

to pub. When the procession reaches the Wiesn, focus switches to the Schottenhamel beer tent and the mayor of Munich who, on the stroke of noon, takes a mallet and knocks the tap into the first keg. As the beer flows forth and the thirsty crowds cheer, the mayor exclaims: *'Ozapft ist's!'* (literally 'It's tapped' in Bavarian dialect). If you want to witness this ceremonial opening of the Oktoberfest, be sure to get there as early as possible.

The Beer

All the lager pulled at Oktoberfest must have been brewed within Munich's city limits, which restricts the number of breweries permitted to wet your whistle to six: Hofbräu-München (of Hofbräuhaus fame), Paulaner, Löwenbräu, Augustiner, and the lesser-known Hacker-Pschorr and Spatenbräu.

GETTING THERE
The nearest metro station to the Oktoberfest venue, the Wiesn, is called Theresienwiese and is served by the U4 and U5, or walk from the Hauptbahnhof.

TOKENS & CASH
No cash changes hands within the beer tents. To get a beer, buy special metal tokens (Biermarken) from outside the tents. Bring lots of cash.

The famous *Mass* (1L mug of beer) brought to your table by a Dirndl-wearing waitress contains pretty strong stuff as the breweries cook up special concoctions for the occasion *(Oktoberfestbier)*. The percentage of alcohol starts at around 5.8%, which makes a single Mass the equivalent of almost 3.5 pints of most regular ales in Britain, Australia and the US. Traditionally the most potent brews are piped to the Wiesn by Hofbräu, the weakest by Hacker-Pschorr.

Away from the Beer Tents

The Oktoberfest is not called the world's biggest fair for nothing, and while most visitors' focus is on the *Bier,* there's a lot going on away from the tents. The funfair with its big wheel, ye-olde

NIKADA/GETTY IMAGES

test-your-strength booths and scarier 21st-century rides are obvious attractions, but magic performances, an agricultural show and stalls selling everything from Oktoberfest souvenirs to waffles constitute other diversions. The first Sunday sees an impressive costumed procession wend its way through Munich city centre, a tradition going back to 1835, and the customary religious Oktoberfest mass is held in the Hippodrom beer tent on the first Thursday. A brass-band concert huffs and puffs beneath the Bavaria statue on the morning of the second Sunday near the spot from where the gun salute is fired on the last Sunday. These events are mostly attended by locals, but give a more traditional insight into the origins and customs of this blockbuster fair.

Fun of the Fair

During the 16 days of festivities, most travellers dip in for a few days, taking time off from the *Mass* to see Munich's sights and perhaps a castle or two.

Part of the fun at the Wiesn is looking the part: traditional Bavarian Dirndl for the gals, Lederhosen and felt hat for the guys. Dirndl consists of a figure-squeezing bodice, a frilly blouse, a skirt that ends just below the knee and an apron. The real deal costs a fortune but Munich has countless discount *Trachten* (folk costume) shops, some of which pop up specially for Oktoberfest, where vastly cheaper versions can be bought or even hired.

The two Tuesdays (until 7pm) are dedicated family days with reduced charges for rides, special family-oriented events, and lots of balloons and roasted almonds. Away from these days, the Augustiner Festhalle is regarded as the most family-friendly beer tent, but children are allowed into all the others. Children can stay in the tents after 8pm but must be accompanied by an adult.

NEED TO KNOW

Where: At the Theresienwiese to the west of the city centre.

When: For 16 days up to the first (occasionally second) Sunday in October.

Opening Hours: Beer is served from 10am to 10.30pm Monday to Friday, 9am to 10.30pm Saturday and Sunday. Other attractions and facilities open longer.

Cost: Admission is free, price of a 1L *Mass* of beer is around €15.

Lake Starnberg

South of Munich and one of several lakes between the city and the Alps, Lake Starnberg is not only a pretty spot to stroll, lunch and escape the central Munich crowds, it is also a place where one of the greatest mysteries of Bavarian history was born.

Starnberg Town

Around 25km southwest of Munich, glittering **Lake Starnberg** (Starnberger See) was once the haunt of Bavaria's royal family but now provides a bit of easily accessible R&R for anyone looking to escape the hustle of the Bavarian capital.

At the northern end of the lake, the S-Bahn drops off just steps from the lake in the affluent town of Starnberg, the northern gateway. On the lakeshore you'll find cruise-boat landing docks, pedal-boat hire and lots of strolling day-trippers.

Mystery at Lake Starnberg

Lake Starnberg may be one of the most attractive retreats south of Munich, but it is also known as a place of tragedy and mystery.

In January 1886 several Bavarian ministers arranged a hasty psychiatric test that diagnosed Ludwig II as mentally unfit to rule. He was dethroned and taken to Schloss Berg on Lake Starnberg. One evening, the dejected royal and his doctor took a lakeside walk and several hours later were found dead – mysteriously drowned in just a few feet of water.

No-one knows with certainty what happened that night. There was no eyewitness or proper criminal investigation. The circumstantial evidence was conflicting and incomplete. Reports and documents were tampered with, destroyed or lost. Conspiracy theories abound.

GETTING THERE
Getting to Lake Starnberg is as easy as boarding the S-Bahn (line S6) at the Hauptbahnhof and alighting in Starnberg 24 minutes later.

Scan for for more information on Starnberg and the Fünf-Seen-Land lake area.

FRANK LAMBERT/SHUTTERSTOCK

An easy 5km hike along the shore takes you to **Berg**, where King Ludwig II spent summers at Schloss Berg and where he and his doctor died. The palace and its lovely gardens still belong to the Wittelsbach family and are closed to prying eyes, but you're free to walk through its wooded park to the **Votivkapelle**. Built in honour of Ludwig and shrouded by mature trees, this neo-Romanesque memorial chapel overlooks the spot in the lake – marked by a simple cross in the water, erected years later by his mother – where Ludwig's dead body was supposedly found.

Fünf-Seen-Land

Lake Starnberg is just one of the lakes in the Fünf-Seen-Land. The others are Ammersee and the much smaller Pilsensee, Wörthsee and Wesslinger See.

QUICK BREAK
On the way from the station to Berg you will pass **Strandhouse** with its lakefront setting and health-conscious menu of bowls, pastas, salads, curries and burgers.

TOOLKIT

Munich Toolkit

Family Travel 142

Accommodation 143

Food, Drink & Nightlife 144

LGBTIQ+ Travellers 146

Health & Safe Travel 147

Responsible Travel 148

Accessible Travel 150

Nuts & Bolts 151

Language 152

Parade for Oktoberfest (p134)
FOOTTOO/GETTY IMAGES©

Family Travel

With its beer halls and Lederhosen, you might consider Munich wholly unsuitable for youngsters. But you'd be wrong. In fact, having kids on board can bring you closer to the locals than lager ever could.

Feeding Time

When it comes to feeding the pack, Germany's south is one of Europe's easier destinations. Most restaurants welcome young diners with smaller portions and special menus. Kids are welcome in beer gardens as long as accompanied by an adult. Chicken schnitzel, sausages, sweet dumplings and strudel are traditional menu items kids will love.

NOT FOR KIDS

Some attractions in Munich come with a warning – unsuitable for children. This applies to the Dachau concentration camp memorial in particular but also to the NS Dokuzentrum and other WWII-related sights.

Discounts

Family tickets are available at the vast majority of sights. It's always worth asking if there's a discount, even if none is advertised. At some of the big-ticket attractions (the Pinakotheken for instance) under 18s get in for free anyway. It's always good to carry photo ID for teenagers who might look older than they actually are.

Pram-friendly

All of Munich's public transport system is pram friendly with lifts down into U-Bahn and S-Bahn stations and low-floored buses and trams.

Breastfeeding

Breastfeeding in public places is perfectly acceptable and many Bavarian women do it.

Public Transport

Children up to six years of age travel free on MVV services. Between six and 14 kids enjoy a heavy discount. A children's single ticket costs €1.90, a day pass just €3.70.

VALENTIN VALKOV/SHUTTERSTOCK

Accommodation

Munich has the full range of accommodation you would expect in a European city, from tents to historic hotels.

Where to Stay if You Love...

History & Shopping

Altstadt (p35) Epicentral place to stay putting you right in the thick of the action with the Marienplatz, the Residenz and Munich's top shopping within walking distance.

Art & Architecture

Maxvorstadt (p61) Puts you amid Munich's Kunstareal with its countless museums and galleries as well as the bustling streets of neighbouring Schwabing.

HOW MUCH FOR A NIGHT IN A

Hostel dorm bed
€32

Boutique midrange hotel **€110**

Central hotel
€150

Best for Budget Stays

Messerstadt Riem

Some 9km east of the Altstadt but easily reachable by U-Bahn, Riem trade fair grounds are the place to seek out bargain accommodation in a city that has become pricey. The trick here is to book a room when there are no events on, as that is when business hotel rates plummet.

Student Nightlife, Offbeat Shopping

Schwabing (p81) The student quarter is packed with bars, restaurants and cafes as well as a few big sights such as the Englischer Garden and the university itself.

Peace & Tranquility

Haidhausen, Lehel & Au (p101) These largely residential neighbourhoods that straddle the Isar are quiet and relaxing but have fewer accommodation options. The Deutsches Museum is nearby.

Cars & Sport

Olympiapark (p115) Staying around the Olympiapark puts you near the BMW complex and the 1972 Olympics venues. Try to find a hotel or Airbnb in the Olympic village.

Food, Drink & Nightlife

⚠ Allergies & Intolerances

People suffering from allergies and intolerances will have few problems eating out in Munich. Any foodstuffs that could cause reactions are normally highlighted on menus. If you suffer from extreme food allergies, speak to your server to make absolutely sure.

HOW TO SAY
I'm allergic to...
Ich bin allergisch gegen...
- **nuts** *Nüsse*
- **seafood** *Meeresfrüchte*
- **dairy products** *Milchprodukte*
- **gluten** *Gluten*

HOW TO ASK...
Is this gluten free?
Ist das glutenfrei?

Does this contain nuts?
Enthält es Nüsse?

Is there a vegan option?
Gibt es etwas für Veganer?

MEAT-FREE & PLANT-BASED

Vegetarians and vegans are relatively well served in the Bavarian capital, with ample dedicated restaurants and options for noncarnivores on every restaurant menu. Even bastions of pork knuckle and schnitzel such as beer halls and beer gardens will offer a couple of token meat-free (though rarely dairy-free) choices.

Beer Garden Dining

There's rarely waiter service at beer gardens – instead order your food and drink at central points. You pay a *Pfand* (deposit; normally €2) for your glass. Carry everything back to the table yourself and when you want more beer, take your tankard back to the serving point.

HOW TO...

Pay the Bill

Asking for the bill Attract the waiter's attention and say *'Zahlen, bitte'*. However most waiters, themselves not German, speak some English.

Splitting the bill The waiter will probably ask if you want to pay together or split the bill. Today it is usually assumed you are paying by card.

Tipping Rounding the final bill up to the nearest five or ten euros is perfectly acceptable, as is giving no tip at all. Never tip huffy or disgruntled service and don't leave cash on tables as you leave as this is considered slightly rude (by Bavarian servers at least).

PRICE RANGES

The following price ranges refer to the average cost of a main course:
€ up to €15
€€ €15–30
€€€ more than €30

OPENING HOURS

Cafes 8am–8pm
Restaurants 11am–10pm
Fast-food joints 11am–midnight

Going Out

Beer halls Most beer halls have waiter service and English menus. Service is usually surprisingly swift and streamlined, even at very busy times. Usually only the beer of the brewery to whom the tavern belongs will be available. Don't sit at the *Stammtisch,* the table reserved for regulars.

Beer gardens Most traditional beer gardens have common features – fairy lights strung between the chestnut trees that shade drinkers from the sun and, for a time at least, summer drizzle. Chairs are slatted and foldable, as are the tables. Order drinks from a central point. Don't picnic at tables set with tablecloths and cutlery. Here also avoid the *Stammtisch!*

Clubs Munich has myriad clubs, from 90s retro to 22nd-century electronic. Door policies range from 'walk in as you like' to 'you'd better be a Bayern Munich player, son'. Don't turn up before midnight or have a train ticket for 5am next day.

HOW MUCH FOR A

Cup of coffee
€3–4

Bottle of water
€1

Scoop of ice cream
€2.50

0.5L of beer
€4–5

Leberkäse sandwich
€3.50

Bratwurst in a bun
€4

Pastry
€2–3

SERGIY KUZMIN/SHUTTERSTOCK

LGBTIQ+ Travellers

Munich has a small but vocal LGBTIQ+ community focused around the Glockenbachviertel south of the Altstadt.

Christopher Street Day

Christopher Street Day is the name by which Gay Pride is often referred to in southern Germany, Austria and Switzerland. Usually taking place in late June, Munich's CSD is a huge event that now takes over almost the entire city with many businesses and attractions getting in on the act with special promotions and the like. Straight or gay, it's a colourful and reassuring time to be in the Bavarian capital and events attract families with children and many rainbow flag–waving heterosexuals who come out in solidarity. The CSD is in fact the culmination of two weeks of LGBTIQ+ community events. The motto for the 2025 Pride Weeks, as they are known, was the catchy *Liberté Diversité Queerité*.

OUR PICKS

Glockenbachviertel

Munich's gay quarter is without doubt the Glockenbachviertel, an area south of the Altstadt. It's here you'll find the majority of gay and lesbian clubs, cafes, hotels and organisations, though they have dispersed slightly over the last decade or so.

GAY OKTOBERFEST

The world's biggest booze-up has for years included events aimed specifically at the gay community. The first Sunday of Oktoberfest is unofficially known as Gay Sunday.

GAY MOUNTAINEERING

A section of the **Deutsche Alpenverein** *(Germany Alpine Club; dav-goc.de)* organises hikes and climbs in the Alps for members of the LGBTIQ+ community. Activities are open to non-members, too, though you may need some German.

CAVAN-IMAGES/SHUTTERSTOCK

Resources

- **munich.travel** Munich's official tourist information portal is one of the best places to go for LGBTIQ+ tourist information.

Health & Safe Travel

Munich is a relatively safe and secure city with a Western healthcare system that's of a very high standard.

OKTOBERFEST
During Oktoberfest crime and staggering drunks are major problems, especially around the Hauptbahnhof. It's no joke: drunks in a crowd trying to make their way home can get violent, and there are around 100 cases of assault every year. Leave early or stay cautious – if not sober – yourself.

Chemists/Pharmacies
Like every central European city, Munich has countless pharmacies that can provide advice and sell over-the-counter medication for nonurgent conditions. This can be preferable (and cheaper) to waiting at a doctors surgery or hospital. They also advise when more specialised help is required and point you in the right direction. If you need medicines for long-term conditions, you may be able to get them using prescriptions from other EU countries though you'll pay the full amount.

Tap Water
Tap water is perfectly safe to drink, but few do. Locals prefer bottled spring and mineral water.

Health Insurance
Citizens of the EU, Switzerland, Iceland, Norway and Liechtenstein receive free or reduced-cost, state-provided (not private) health care with their European Health Insurance Card (EHIC). Brits need a GHIC (Global Health Insurance Card). Each family member needs a separate card. All other visitors should ideally take out full travel/health insurance or be prepared to pay.

BICYCLE LANES

Heavy, fast-moving e-bikes in central Munich are a menace. Make sure you don't wander onto bike lanes, especially when waiting to cross the road.

QUICK INFO

Inebriation
Puts you at risk, especially late at night on public transport.

Lock bicycles
Always; preferably choose a high-traffic area.

Phone snatching
Rare but on the increase.

Responsible Travel

Follow these tips to leave a lighter footprint, support local and have a positive impact on communities.

The Pfand
When buying drinks in a shop, count on the fact that you'll pay a deposit *(Pfand)* when you buy certain bottles and cans. When you return the empty, you get your deposit back and the container is recycled. Deposits are between 10 and 25 cents and you can return bottles at any shop that sells them. Note that not all bottles have a deposit, but they can still be recycled.

Get Educated
Those with a deeper interest in Munich's commitment to a sustainable future should arrange a visit to the **Ökologisches Bildungszentrum** *(Ecological Education Centre; oebz.de)* in the Bogenhausen district of the city.

FROM LEFT: IL21/GETTY IMAGES, PROONTY/SHUTTERSTOCK

Oktoberfest
By simply banning single-use plates and cutlery and certain drinks containers, Oktoberfest has reduced its waste by hundreds of tons.

Sustainable Shopping
Munich provides lots of opportunities to buy high-quality secondhand clothes, as well as used traditional costume for Oktoberfest. **Pick n Weight** *(picknweight.de/pages/munich)*, **Holareidulijö** *(holareidulijoe.com)* and **Oxfam** *(oxfam.de)* are just some of the places you can pick up pre-worn garb.

Resources
- **wwf.de** Germany's WWF website with lots of info and volunteering opportunities.
- **aktion-deutschland-hilft.de** Find out how you can help Ukrainian and other refugees in southern Germany.
- **munich.travel** Has a large sustainable travel section.

---------- **STAYING GREEN** ----------

On the **Germany tourism website** *(germany.travel)* you can check the green credentials of almost 400 accommodation providers across Germany. These are hotels with Green Sign certification or other sustainability awards.

Ambitious Targets

Munich has set itself some pretty ambitious sustainability targets concerning carbon neutrality, emissions and waste management. The city is committed to carbon neutrality by 2035, a full decade earlier than the rest of Germany. Munich also aims to reduce emissions by 50% compared to 1990 levels by 2030.

City Hall is also trying to implement a zero waste strategy, using geothermal heating systems, decarbonising buildings, and investing in shared mobility infrastructure. While these goals are admirable, the strain on local businesses and administrations charged with finding solutions to almost impossible problems is huge.

GREENWASH

Bavaria is awash with 'greenwash' as businesses struggle with tricky and expensive sustainability targets. It is always a good idea to check any environmentally friendly claims businesses make if you can. Accommodation providers are the biggest culprits.

Climate Change & Travel

It's impossible to ignore the impact we have when travelling; Lonely Planet urges all travellers to engage with their travel carbon footprint, which will mainly come from air travel. While there often isn't an alternative, travellers can look to minimise the number of flights they take, opt for newer aircrafts and use cleaner ground transport, such as trains. One proposed solution – purchasing carbon offsets – unfortunately does not cancel out the impact of individual flights. While most destinations will depend on air travel for the foreseeable future, for now, pursuing ground-based travel where possible is the best course of action.

The **UN Carbon Offset Calculator** shows how flying impacts a household's emissions

The **ICAO's carbon emissions calculator** allows visitors to analyse the CO2 generated by point-to-point journeys

Accessible Travel

Accommodation

Upper-end and midrange hotels should be barrier free though may have only a single room for wheelchair users. All hotels and guesthouses should be able to tell you in advance whether their property is suitable. Beware claims by Airbnb hosts that their property has disabled access only to find eight flights of stairs to the door.

Guided Tours

The **Munich tourist office** *(munich.travel)* arranges barrier-free guided tours of the city centre for travellers with disabilities. These can be booked by calling the office and last between two and three hours. Prices are relatively high.

Of all of Munich's myriad attractions, **BMW Welt** (p123) is top of the league when it comes to barrier-free access. Those in wheelchairs can access every single part of the building with level entrances, ramps and lifts at all strategic points. The layout of the exhibition is sufficiently spacious (though we did notice the odd step up to some cars) and there are barrier-free toilets and cafe facilities. If you do encounter issues, staff are on hand to help.

CITY TRANSPORT

The whole MVV system is barrier free and you should have no problem boarding buses, trams and the U-Bahn. Allow time at S-Bahn stations to use the lifts, which can be very slow.

Equipment Rental

For wheelchair and scooter rental plus any other equipment you may need, the most central point to turn to is **Von Schlieben** *(von schlieben.de)* at Karlsplatz/Stachus, which offers a full service.

--- **BEER GARDENS** ---

Munich's beer gardens are some of the best places for those with disabilities to eat and drink as they are by their nature open and barrier free.

Resources

● **kultur-barrierefrei-muenchen.de** Munich Accessible Culture website dedicated to helping those with disabilities enjoy culture in the Bavarian capital.

Nuts & Bolts

Opening Hours
Supermarkets across Germany can only open on Sunday if they are located in a train station, airport or other transport terminal.

Banks 9.30am–5pm Monday–Friday, some to 1pm Saturday

Bars 5pm–1am or later

Cafes 8am–8pm

Clubs 11pm–4am or later

Post Offices 9am–6pm Monday–Friday, to 1pm Saturday

Restaurants 11am–11pm

Shops 9am–8pm Monday–Saturday

Supermarkets 8am–7pm Mon–Sat

QUICK INFO
Time zone CET
City calling code 89
Emergency number 112
Population 1.6 million

ELECTRICITY

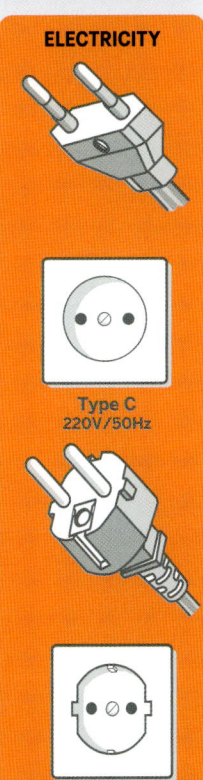

Type C
220V/50Hz

Type F
230V/50Hz

Public Holidays
Businesses and offices are closed on the following public holidays:

Neujahrstag (New Year's Day) 1 January

Heilige Drei Könige (Epiphany) 6 January

Ostern (Easter) March/April Good Friday, Easter Sunday and Easter Monday

Maifeiertag (Labour Day) 1 May

Christi Himmelfahrt (Ascension Day) 40 days after Easter

Pfingsten (Whitsun/Pentecost) mid-May to mid-June – Whit Sunday and Whit Monday

Fronleichnam (Corpus Christi) 10 days after Pentecost

Mariä Himmelfahrt (Assumption Day) 15 August

Tag der Deutschen Einheit (Day of German Unity) 3 October

Weihnachtstag (Christmas Day) 25 December

Zweiter Weihnachtstag (Second Day of Christmas) 26 December

Toilets
Public toilets are rarely free. Rather irritating Sanifair barriered paid toilets are even being installed in shopping centres and train stations (these give a voucher for use in the location they are situated). They cost up to €1 and aren't always in the best condition.

Language

German Basics

Hello.
Guten Tag. *goo·ten tahk*

Goodbye.
Auf Wiedersehen. *owf vee·der·zay·en*

Yes.
Ja. *yah*

No.
Nein. *nain*

Please.
Bitte. *bi·te*

Thank you.
Danke. *dang·ke*

You're welcome.
Bitte. *bi·te*

Excuse me/sorry.
Entschuldigung. *ent·shul·di·gung*

Fast Phrases

Do you speak English?
Sprechen Sie Englisch? (pol) *shpre·khen zee eng·lish*
Sprichst du Englisch? (inf) *shprikhst doo eng·lish*

I don't understand.
Ich verstehe nicht. *ikh fer·shtay·e nikht*

I'd like... **Ich möchte...** *ikh merkh·te...*
  a beer. **ein Bier.** *ain beer*
  a coffee. **einen Kaffee.** *ai·nen ka·fay*
  a white wine. **ein Glas Weisswein.** *ain·glahs vais·vain*
  a red wine. **ein Glas Rotwein.** *ain·glahs rawt·vain*

The bill, please.
Die Rechnung, bitte. *dee rekh·nung bi·te*

How much is this?
Wie viel kostet das? *vee feel kos·tet das*

Where's the toilet?
Wo ist die Toilette? *vo ist dee to·a·le·te*

Please speak more slowly.
Könnten Sie bitte langsamer sprechen? *kern·ten zee bi·te lang·za·mer shpre·khen*

Where's the nearest ATM?
Wo ist der nächste Geldautomat? *vaw ist dair naykhs·te gelt·ow·to·maht*

Could I have a receipt, please?
Könnte ich eine Quittung bekommen? *kern·te ikh ai·ne kvi·tung be·ko·men*

Numbers

  eins *ains*

 zwei *tsvai*

 drei *drai*

 vier *feer*

 fünf *fünf*

Good to Know

German words can have different **endings**, depending on their role in the sentence. There's also a formal and informal word for 'you' (*Sie* and *du*, respectively).

The two dots that sometimes appear above the vowels a, o and u are called **umlauts** and affect how words are pronounced. You'll see them in words like *Bäckerei* (bakery), *Löffel* (spoon) and *Frühstück* (breakfast).

In German, the **ß** character is called **eszett**. It's used in Straße, the word for street, and in the expletive Scheiße. It's often transliterated as 'ss'.

WORDS WITHIN WORDS

Don't be put off by the fact that German tends to join words together to express a single notion – it's not hard to tell parts of words, and you'll have fun recognising 'the Football World Cup qualifying match' hidden within *Fussballweltmeisterschaftsqualifikationsspiel*!

Signs
- **Ausgang** Exit
- **Eingang** Entrance
- **Offen** Open
- **Geschlossen** Closed
- **Damen** Women
- **Herren** Men
- **Toiletten (WC)** Toilets
- **Hauptbahnhof** Main train station
- **Flughafen** Airport
- **Strasse (Str.)** Street
- **Ziehen** Pull
- **Drucken** Push
- **Rauchen verboten** No Smoking

Listen for
Ihren Reisepass, bitte. *ee·ren rai·ze·pas bi·te*
Your passport, please.
Ihr Visum, bitte. *eer vee·zum bi·te*
Your visa, please.

--- SOUND LIKE A LOCAL ---

Hey! Hey! *hei*
Great! Toll! *tol*
Cool! Spitze! *shpi·tse*
No problem. Kein Problem. *kain pro·blaym*
Sure. Klar! *klahr*
Maybe. Vielleicht. *fi·laikht*
No way! Auf keinen Fall! *owf kai·nen fal*
It's OK. Alles klar. *a·les klahr*

 sechs *zeks* 6

 sieben *zee·ben* 7

 acht *akht* 8

 neun *noyn* 9

 zehn *tsayn* 10

Index

Sights 000   Map pages 000

See also separate subindexes for:
- **Eating p156**
- **Drinking p157**
- **Shopping p157**

A

accessible travel 150
accommodation 25, 143, 149
Afghan cuisine 30-1
Ainmillerstrasse 91
airports 26
Akademie der Bildenden Künste 92
allergies, food 144
Alte Pinakothek 64
Alter Botanischer Garten 73, 74
Alter Hof 49
Alter Nordfriedhof 73
Altes Rathaus 43
Altes Schloss Schleissheim 96-7
Altstadt 35-59, **36-7**
  accommodation 143
  drinking 56-7
  experiences 50-3
  food 54-6
  itineraries 48-9, **48**
  shopping 58-9
  top experiences 38-47
  transport 35
  walking tours 48-9, **48**
Amalienstrasse 91
architecture 14-15, 30
arriving in Munich 26
art galleries 8-9
Asamkirche 44-5
Au 101-13, **102-3**
  accommodation 143
  experiences 110-11
  food 112-13
  itineraries 108-9, **108**
  top experiences 104-7
  transport 101
  walking tours 108-9, **108**
Auer Dult 25
Auer Mühlbach 109
Augustenstrasse 73

B

bathrooms 151
Bayerisches Nationalmuseum 89
Bayerisches Nationaltheater 49
beer halls & gardens 6-7, 10, 144-5
  Augustiner Keller 77
  Augustiner Stammhaus 49, 56
  Biergarten Muffatwerk 109, 113
  Braunauer Hof 57
  Chinesischer Turm 85, 95
  Der Pschorr 56-7
  Hirschau 95
  Hirschgarten 133
  Hofbräuhaus 47, 49
  Hofbräukeller 113
  Löwenbräukeller 77
  Park Cafe 76
  Paulaner am Nockherberg 109, 113
  Tegernseer Tal 56
  Viktualienmarkt 57
Berlin Wall 86
bicycle travel 28, 29, 87, 111
Bier & Oktoberfestmuseum 50-1
BMW 115-17, 123-6, 133, **116-17**
BMW Museum 124-6
BMW Plant 126
BMW Welt 123-4, 150
Bonifaz Church 73
bookings 22
breastfeeding 142
budget 17, 23, see also costs
bus travel 26, 28, 74
business hours 145, 151

C

car travel 28
chemists 147
children, travel with 17, 142
Chinesischer Turm 85, 95
Christmas markets 24, 42, 51
Christopher Street Day 146
climate 24
climate change 149
clubs 145
costs 23
  accommodation 143
  drinks 145
  food 145
  transport 29
currency 23
Cuvilliés-Theater 41
cycling 28, 29, 87, 111

D

Dachau 78-9
dangers 87, 147
de Cuvilliés, François 41
DenkStätte Weisse Rose 88
Deutsches Museum 104-5
Deutsches Museum - Verkehrszentrum 105
Dirndl 58, 77, 137
disabilities, travellers with 150
drinking 144-5, see also individual neighbourhoods, Drinking subindex
driving 28
drunkenness 147

E

Eisbachwelle 86, 87
electricity 151
emergencies 151
Englischer Garten 84-7
environmental issues 148-9
e-scooters 29
etiquette 22
events 24-5

F

family travel 17, 142
Feldherrnhalle 51-2

festivals 24-5
Flugwerft Schleissheim 97
food 144-5, *see also individual neighbourhoods*, Eating subindex
   Afghan cuisine 30-1
   Weisswurst 50
Franz Josef Strauss Airport 26
Frauenkirche 46
free attractions 17
Friedensengel 110
Frühlingsfest 24

G
galleries 8-9
gay travellers 52, 146
German language 152-3
Glockenbachviertel 146
Glockenspiel 42
green spaces 30
greenwashing 149

H
Haidhausen 101-13, **102-3**
   accommodation 143
   experiences 110-11
   food 112-13
   itineraries 108-9, **108**
   top experiences 104
   transport 101
   walking tours 108-9, **108**
Haidhausen Cemetery 109
Hauptbahnhof 26
Haus der Kunst 92
health 147
Heiliggeistkirche 52
highlights 6-17
   Altstadt 38-47
   Au 104-7
   Haidhausen 104
   Lehel 104-7
   Maxvorstadt 64-71
   Schwabing 84-9
history
   1972 Olympics 120-1
   former Munich sites 31
   Jewish history 50
   Nazis 50, 70-1, 92
   WWII sites 16, 50, 70-1, 78-9, 107
Hitler, Adolf 70-1
Hofbräuhaus 47, 49
Hofgarten 52
holidays 151

I
insurance, health 147
itineraries 18-21, *see also individual neighbourhoods*

J
Jewish history 50
Jüdisches Museum 50
Justizpalast 75

K
Karlsplatz 49
Kinderreich 104-5
Kino am Olympiasee 131
Klosterkirche St Anna im Lehel 111
Königsplatz 67-8
Kriechbaumhof 109
Kunstareal 64-9
KZ-Gedenkstätte Dachau 78-9

L
Lake Starnberg 138-9
language 152-3
Lederhosen 58, 77, 137
Lehel 101-13, **102-3**
   accommodation 143
   experiences 110-11
   food 112-13
   top experiences 104-7
   transport 101
Lenbachhaus 68
Leopoldpark 91
Leuchtenberg-Palais 93
LGBTIQ+ travellers 52, 146
Ludwig-Maximilians-Universität 88, 91
Ludwigskirche 92

M
Mariahilfplatz 109
Marienplatz 42-3
Marstallmuseum 129
Maximilianeum 110
Maximilianstrasse 49
Maxvorstadt 61-77, **62-3**
   accommodation 143
   drinking 76-7
   experiences 74-5
   food 76
   itineraries 72-3, **72**
   shopping 77
   top experiences 64-71

   transport 61, 74
   walking tours 72-3, **72**
Messerstadt Riem 143
Michael Jackson Shrine 49
Michaelskirche 49
money 23
Monument to the Victims of National Socialism 50
motorcycle travel 28
Müller'sches Volksbad 109
Münchner Kammerspiele 53
Münchner Marionettentheater 53
Munich Film Festival 25
Munich Marathon 25
Munich Residenz 38-41, 40
Munich Technical University 73
Museum Brandhorst 65-6
Museum der Bayerischen Könige 99
Museum Fünf Kontinente 110
Museum Mensch und Natur 129
Museum Villa Stuck 106
museums 12-13
music
   classical 111
   festivals 24
   opera 49, 53

N
Nationaltheater 53
Nazis 50, 70-1, 92
Neue Pinakothek 69
Neues Rathaus 42
Neues Schloss Schleissheim 96
nightlife 144-5
Nordbad 73
NS Dokuzentrum 70-1
Nymphenburg 115, 127-9, **116-17**
   drinking 133
   food 132-3
   transport 115

O
Oktoberfest 24, 134-7, 146, 147, 148
Olympic village 121, 131
Olympiaberg 119
Olympiapark 115-22, 116-17
   accommodation 143
   itineraries 130-1, **130**
   transport 115
   walking tours 130-1, **130**

Olympiasee 131
Olympiastadion 118
Olympiaturm 118-19
opening hours 145, 151
Ost-West Friedenskirche 121, 131

P

parks 30, 74, 84-5
Pfand 148
pharmacies 147
Pinakothek der Moderne 66-7
planning 22-3
  booking 22
  etiquette 22
  Munich basics 22-3
  tips 22
population 151
prams 142
Pride Weeks 52
Prinzregententheater 111
public holidays 151
public transport 27-9

R

recycling 148
Residenz, the 38-41, **40**
Residenztheater 53
responsible travel 148-9
ride shares 28

S

safe travel 147
Sammlung Schack 110-11
SAP Garden 131
S-Bahn 26, 27, 28-9
Schellingstrasse 91
Schleissheim 96-7
Schloss Hohenschwangau 98
Schloss Lustheim 96-7
Schloss Neuschwanstein 98-9
Schloss Nymphenburg 127-9
Scholl, Hans & Sophie 88, 93
Schwabing 81-95, **82-3**
  accommodation 143
  experiences 92-3
  food 94-5
  itineraries 90-1, **90**
  top experiences 84-9
  transport 81
  walking tours 90-1, **90**
Sea Life 122

shopping 11, *see also individual neighbourhoods,* Shopping *subindex*
Siegestor 93
St Bonifaz Church 75
St Joseph Church 73
St Nikolaikirche 111
St Peterskirche 43
St Ursulakirche 93
Staatstheater am Gärtnerplatz 53
Starkbierzeit 25
Starnberg 138-9
State Museum of Egyptian Art 74
Sudetendeutsches Museum 107
surfing 86, 87
surprises 30-1
sustainability 148-9

T

telephone codes 151
Theater im Marstall 53
Theatinerkirche 52-3
theatres 41, 53
theft 147
time 23
tipping 23, 144
toilets 151
Tollwood Summer Festival 24
Trachten 58, 77, 137
train travel 26, 27
trams 27-8
transport 26, 27-9
travel seasons 24-5
travelling with children 17, 142

U

U-Bahn 27, 28-9
Uber 26, 28

V

vegetarian & vegan travellers 144
  restaurants 55, 76
  vegan clothing 95
Viktualienmarkt 53
von Gärtner, Friedrich 30

W

walking tours
  Altstadt 48-9, **48**
  Au 108-9, **108**
  Haidhausen 108-9, **108**
  Maxvorstadt 72-3, **72**
  Olympiapark 130-1, **130**
  Schwabing 90-1, **90**
water 147
weather 24
Wedekind-Platz 91
Weisse Rose Movement 88, 93
Weisses Bräuhaus 50
Weisswurst 50
Wiener Platz 109
WWII sites 16, 50, 70-1, 78-9, 107

Z

Zentraler Omnibusbahnhof 26

 Eating

A

Alois - Dallmayr Fine Dining 56
Andechser am Dom 54
Augustiner Stammhaus 54
Ayinger in der Au 112

B

Bavarie by Käfer 133
Biker's Lodge 125
Bohemia München 112
Bratwurstherzl 54

C

Cadu (Cafe an der Uni) 94
Cafe Exponat 113
Café Glockenspiel 54
Cafe Ignaz 76
Cafe Luitpold 56
Café Romanplat 133
Cafe Zeitgeist 94
Chopan 133
Chopan - Gasteig 112

D

Der Sizilianer 112
Die Vegane Fleischerei 55

E

Einstein 55
Eiscafé Sarcletti 132
Emmi's Kitchen 94

F
Fischhäusl 113
Fräulein Grüneis 94
Fraunhofer 54

G
Galleria 55-6
Götterspeise 54

H
Hewad 55

I
Il Mulino 76
Indian Love Story 55

J
Jan 76

K
Kainz Restaurant 99

L
Le Stollberg 56
Les Deux 56

M
Münchner Suppenküche 56

N
NIGIN 55

P
Prinz Myshkin 55

R
Ruffini 132
Ruff's Burger (Occamstrasse) 94
Ruff's Burger (Rindermarkt) 55

S
Sankt Annas 76
Schall & Rauch 94-5
Schlosscafé im Palmenhaus 132
Schlosswirtschaft Oberschleißheim 97
Schmalznudel 54
Schoberwirt 112

Schumanns Tagesbar 56
Secret Garden 55
Showroom 112
Steinheil 16 76
Strandhouse 139
Swagat 112

T
Tantris 94
Tohru 56
Türkenhof 94

W
Weinhaus Neuner 55
Weisses Bräuhaus 50, 54
Werksviertel 113
Werneckhof 94
Wirtshaus in der Au 112
Wirtshaus Obacht 76

Z
Zauberberg 133
Zum Dürnbräu 54-5

 Drinking

Alter Simpl 76
Augustiner Keller 77
Augustiner Stammhaus 49, 56
Baader Café 57
Biergarten Muffatwerk 109
Braunauer Hof 57
Cadu (Cafe an der Uni) 88
Cafe Jasmin 77
Cafe Pini 57
Chinesischer Turm 85, 95
Cocktailhouse 95
Der Pschorr 56-7
Die Kneipe 80 77
Goldene Bar 95
Hermanns 113
Hirschau 95
Hirschgarten 133

Hofbräukeller 113
Japanisches Teehaus 86-7
Löwenbräukeller 77
Park Cafe 76
Paulaner am Nockherberg 109, 113
Pils Doktor 95
Tegernseer Tal 56
Trachtenvogl 57
Viktualienmarkt 57

 Shopping

Bottles & Glashaus 58
Capricorn Store 59
Daller Tracht 77
Dear Goods 95
Deutsches Museum Shop 113
FC Bayern World 58
Flohmarkt Olympiapark 131
Fünf Höfe 59
Galeria Kaufhof Marienplatz 58
Globetrotter 58
Gössl 58
Holareidulijö 77
Inntaler Trachtenwelt 58
Kunst Oase 95
Kustermann 58
Loden-Frey 58
Ludwig Beck 58
Macy 113
Manufactum 58
Munich Readery 77
Picknweight 59
Porzellan Manufaktur Nymphenburg 129
Schrannenhalle 59
Schuster 58
Stachus Passagen 59
Viktualienmarkt 59
Vintage Etcetera 113
Words' Worth Books 95

Send Us Your Feedback

We love to hear from travellers – your comments help make our books better. We read every word, and we guarantee that your feedback goes straight to the authors. Visit lonelyplanet.com/contact to submit your updates and suggestions.

Note: We may edit, reproduce and incorporate your comments in Lonely Planet products such as guidebooks, websites and digital products, so let us know if you are happy to have your name acknowledged. For a copy of our privacy policy visit lonelyplanet.com/legal.

Acknowledgements

Cover photograph: Neues Rathaus and Marienplatz. Nikada/Getty Images

Back photograph: Viktualienmarkt. trabantos/Shutterstock

THIS BOOK

This 3rd edition of Lonely Planet's Pocket Munich guidebook was researched and written by Marc Di Duca. The previous edition was also written by Marc Di Duca. This guidebook was produced by the following:

Destination Editor
Sandie Kestell

Production Editor
Sasha Drew

Cartographer
Anita Hang Banh

Image Editor
Lyn Horst

Assisting Editor
Fionnuala Twomey

Cover Researcher
Daisy Korpics

Thanks to
Hannah Cartmel, Fergal Condon, Wayne Murphy, Charlotte Orr

Although the authors and Lonely Planet have taken all reasonable care in preparing this book, we make no warranty about the accuracy or completeness of its content and, to the maximum extent permitted, disclaim all liability arising from its use.

All rights reserved. No part of this publication may be copied, stored in a retrieval system, or transmitted in any form by any means, electronic, mechanical, recording or otherwise, except brief extracts for the purpose of review, and no part of this publication may be sold or hired, without the written permission of the publisher. Lonely Planet and the Lonely Planet logo are trademarks of Lonely Planet and are registered in the US Patent and Trademark Office and in other countries. Lonely Planet does not allow its name or logo to be appropriated by commercial establishments, such as retailers, restaurants or hotels. Please let us know of any misuses: lonelyplanet.com/legal/intellectual-property.

Paper in this book is certified against the Forest Stewardship Council™ standards. FSC™ promotes environmentally responsible, socially beneficial and economically viable management of the world's forests.

Published by Lonely Planet Global Limited
CRN 554153
3rd edition – Apr 2026
ISBN 978 1 83758 434 5
© Lonely Planet 2026
10 9 8 7 6 5 4 3 2 1
Printed in China